WILD LIFE

50 projects to rewild your life
from the home to outdoors

Hardie Grant

EXPLORE

FOR MY CAMPING FAMILY
NICK, TASMAN, FREYA, KATE, BILL, ZARA, SASHA, WILLOW,
KYLIE, CARL, SASKIA, MIKO, GRETA, CAM, DASH, JET,
BELINDA, LUCAS, MAX & ALEX

LOVE ANNA X

Anna Carlile is the founder of Design by Nature, a creative studio in Melbourne, Australia that draws inspiration from nature and promotes design which celebrates and protects the environment. This book was brought together by the passion and dedication of Anna with designers Megan Edgoose and Kristin Soh, and wordsmiths Vanessa Murray and Georgia Gibson.

Design by Nature acknowledges and respects the Traditional Custodians and their deep and continuing spiritual connection to the land and waters, and their Elders past and present, whose knowledge and wisdom has ensured the continuation of culture and traditional practices and their unique ability and ongoing role in caring for Country.

Design by Nature

INNER LIFE

HOME LIFE

NEIGHBOURHOOD LIFE

FOREST LIFE

RIVER LIFE

COAST LIFE

INTRODUCTION

Wild Life celebrates the moments that make me feel most alive, most human. Many of the projects are aspirational; they are what I aspire to learn to be more connected with our land and to feel more confident and comfortable when I'm off-grid out in the wild. I want to be able to find north, identify food to forage and eat, swim in wild rivers, hike on multi-day trips with just my pack and camp under the big, open night sky. These are the kind of adventures I love to plan and have.

In my urban life of Brunswick, an inner-suburb of Melbourne, I chase the green spaces. My bedroom looks out over gum trees and a small park we share with a community of 10 mirror households. It is where we gather as a community to share time together in nature, feast, have bonfires to celebrate winter solstice and share raising our children. A bike trail winding along the local Merri Creek connects me with our design studio and the mighty and iconic Melbourne river, the Yarra. Majestic gums tower along the banks and fruit bats make their pilgrimage each night to feast, filling the evening sky. Nestled in an arts community at the Abbotsford Convent and next to the Collingwood Children's Farm, our creative studio Design by Nature is surrounded by green and overlooks trees and we can hear the sound of sheep bleating in the paddocks outside – while only 3km from the city centre, it feels like the countryside.

May this book inspire you to live a wild life, a connected life where our collective small steps of change lead to a future of change, where our urban spaces regenerate and where we live in balance with nature and our true selves.

Through six carefully considered and curated sections, this book invites you to step back, take a breath and start to rewild your life. Read in a linear fashion from start to finish, *Wild Life* takes you on a journey that begins with the self, goes through the home and out to the neighbourhood, then even further into the wild places of forest, river and coast. You can journey through each chapter in order or dip in and out as your mood and inclination take you. That's the beauty of the rewilding journey: you can do it your way.

It's time to rewild.

Anna x

LIVING A WILD LIFE

Living a wild life doesn't mean you have to quit your day job and move out of the city to live on a self-sustainable farm or that you have to sleep in a cave or eat suspicious mushrooms from the forest floor, although you can learn to do all of these well if you want to. Simply put, it's about acknowledging and feeding your innate, age-old desire to be in and to connect with nature — to rewild.

The original meaning of the term 'rewilding' is to restore an area of land to its natural, uncultivated state, but in more recent years, the term has also been applied to humankind — people living largely modern, urbanised lives who actively seek to reconnect with nature and live a simpler, more sustainable and harmonious way of life. It involves reinstating once wild ecosystems with native, biodiverse flora and fauna, and one formidable example is the extraordinary sequence of events that happened with the reintroduction of wolves into Yellowstone National Park in 1995. Absent for over 70 years, wolves were returned to the park to control the deer populations, which were over-grazing and destroying the park. Less deer led to flourishing greenery, which encouraged birds and beavers to return. The beavers created dams in the rivers where reptiles and fish were thriving, and the regeneration of the forests strengthened the riverbanks, making the river ways more resilient and reliable. By rewilding just one piece of the puzzle — the wolves — an entire ecosystem was returned to the harmonious state that it intelligently evolved over millions of years to become.

For hundreds of thousands of years, our human ancestors lived a truly wild and free life — a life that evolved to be wholly reliant on and interconnected with nature. They hunted and foraged for their food and built shelters in the wilderness. They started to develop tools from materials found in their environment, and they learnt how to control the element of fire and to use it to their advantage. Nature has always been our home and our guide. Instigated perhaps by our natural curiosity and sense of adventure, it is from observing nature and everything around us — plants, animals, tides, clouds and celestial bodies alike — that we've learnt to navigate the land and the seas to discover and better understand the world around us. We evolved in nature and our bodies and senses were created to thrive in it, forging an inherent connection with the natural elements that is still present in us today.

Over the last couple of centuries, the way we live has seen drastic changes, as technology and, recently, electronics have started to rule our lives. Suddenly, all of our needs are met with little effort on our part, and we have machines to do the work for us, or, at the very least, make tasks easier. We've got machines that can take us and all the products we are encouraged to continuously consume from A to B; machines that sow, harvest and process the food we eat; and now we even have machines that — while small enough to fit in a pocket — contains the entire online universe and are readily available to transfix us at the slightest hint of boredom. Our modern lifestyle has changed our relationship with nature, and we now spend the majority of our lives indoors, increasingly sedentary and absorbed in at least one screen. We've become domesticated. The lights from our cities are fading out the stars, traffic noises are drowning out birdsong and the rustle of wind in the trees and the tall buildings are obscuring and blocking our view of the expanse beyond the concrete stretching towards the horizon. The homes we live in and lives we need no longer revolve around nature, and it seems like the constant noise and lights of modern life are dulling our senses and natural instincts. With this detachment from the environment came decades of ruthless extraction of natural resources to feed all of our machines – especially the insatiable and avaricious 'machine of economic growth'. This disconnect from the natural world, from our wild selves, has led us into a world of environmental degradation and declining human health, and many of us have lost our connection to ourselves, too. Our environment is suffering and our health, not least our mental health, is suffering – but this doesn't have to be our story.

Increasingly, humans are starting to understand that our inherent connection to our wild selves and wild places is vital for our health and presence on Earth. We are starting to discover and understand that nurturing and strengthening our inherent connection with nature has multiple benefits, not just for our planet but also for our health and wellbeing.

Consider this. Within a few minutes of being in green spaces, our brains start to calm down and we experience a sense of wellbeing. Our nervous system relaxes, our digestion is better supported, our energy restores and our heart rate and blood pressure lower. After half an hour in nature, our stress hormone, cortisol, drops, improving our immune system, blood sugar levels, memory and brain function. In Canada, doctors can even prescribe annual passes to national parks as part of treatment plans, and they hope that the initiative will also help fight climate change, as the more time people spend in nature, the more likely they are to protect it. By turning off our devices, returning to the wild and tapping into our senses, we can start rebuilding our bond with the natural environment and reap the health and planetary benefits that will come with it.

It makes sense, doesn't it? After all, we've spent millennia evolving outside in forests and prairies and caves, mapping our lives around the waxing and waning of the moon, the paths of rivers and streams and the give and take of the seasons and, in Earth terms, only the blink of an eye in our industrial and technologically advanced world. We come from stars and dust, and our bodies are filled with salt water, and we've spent millennia evolving to survive in most of the natural environments on every corner of Earth, so it's no wonder we thrive when we immerse ourselves in the natural world. Nature provides the air we breathe, the food we eat and the materials to create shelter and warmth. Nature provides endless beauty all around

X

us throughout its cycles and seasons, from sunsets and mountain vistas to the flowers in your neighbours' front yards and the little wildflower, so often called a weed, that has somehow, by sheer determination and bravery one would imagine, broken through the concrete path to make the sidewalk its home. Now more than ever, we also need to look out for our beautiful planet, as those who value greed and power higher than human health and lives continue their ruthless extraction, destroying everything in their path. Just as adding one piece of the puzzle re-established the ecosystem in Yellowstone, removing pieces of the puzzle can make these fragile systems collapse, too. Nature is teaching us that diversity is a good thing and that sometimes the best thing we can do is take a step back and let nature heal its own wounds. While we are here, evolving with and living off the Earth and her abundance, the least we can do is our very best to make sure we don't lose any puzzle pieces in the process.

When we rewild ourselves, we also choose to create a better future. We rehone our senses and instincts, reclaim our creativity and live in a way that is as nourishing, grounded and mindful of the world and all its inhabitants as possible. We already have much of the knowledge we need to turn things in a greener direction, and our technological advances have given us ways to harvest renewable resources to fuel our modern lifestyle, such as wind, sun and water – interestingly, all elements you are encouraged to seek out in the rewilding projects throughout this book.

Wild Life is your permission to disconnect from one world to reconnect with another; to put down your devices and pick up where your wild self left off. Be guided by your curiosity and inspired to engage with the natural elements on your own rewilding journey. You don't have to get your nails dirty if you don't want to (although we highly encourage you to, as soil under your fingernails has its own health benefits), and hopefully the pages before you will motivate you to explore the natural environment in your own way and at your own pace. Perhaps you prefer to start by tuning into your senses and practise mindfulness in your everyday life, or perhaps you're ready to take the plunge and fully submerge yourself in a cold body of water or head off-grid for an overnight hike or camping trip. Live life as wild as you want (or dare!), but live life wild and free.

XI

"ALL GOOD
THINGS
ARE WILD
AND FREE."

HENRY DAVID THOREAU
WALKING

INNER

LIFE

TUNE
INTO YOUR
SENSES

The sound of rustling trees, the smell of fresh rain and the sight of a sunset are all examples of natural things that can ground us in the moment. By being mindful and tuning into our senses, we can guide our minds away from worrying about the past or future and instead simply enjoy living in the now.

When we focus on our senses, we help our brain shift from a place of underlying worry and stress towards one of presence, intention and content. As you breathe, start to tune into your five senses — sight, sound, smell, taste and touch — one at a time.

What do you hear? Listen as intentionally as you can. Perhaps you can hear birds or waves or the hum of traffic. What do you smell? How does the sun, the breeze or the fabric you're wearing feel on your skin? What can you taste? What scents can you detect? If you're in nature, look deeply at the movement of the leaves in the trees or the way the sun plays on water.

In everyday life, focus on a simple act, like making a pot of tea. Pay close attention to the actions, moments and sensory experiences that are part of creating it: taking your teapot by the handle and feeling the touch of its cool ceramic surface as you pick it up, the sound of scooping up the tea leaves, the sound and sensation of pouring water into the pot and so on.

Here are some simple techniques to help you tune into your senses and slow down.

MINDFULNESS AND MEDITATION

In recent years, the Western world has been increasingly drawn to mindfulness and meditation as a means of calming our minds, connecting with our bodies and slowing down. What's the difference? At a fundamental level, mindfulness can be defined as the awareness of 'some-thing' while meditation is the awareness of 'no-thing'. They're symbiotic — mindfulness supports and enriches meditation, while meditation nurtures and expands mindfulness. Mindfulness can be applied at any given moment throughout the day, while meditation is usually practised in a specific place or posture for a specific amount of time. When we meditate or practise mindfulness, we soften mental noise, release pressure on our muscles and calm our nervous system.

PAUSE AND RECALIBRATE

Ultimately, being mindful is about pausing and consciously relaxing and softening our minds and bodies. To truly slow ourselves down, we must recalibrate — shift our thinking and way of being from a hectic, fast-paced modern lifestyle to one that is slower and more in tune with nature. The mindful and meditative breathing technique (*see* page 6) quite literally slows your heartbeat and is a great first step in recalibrating. You really can do it anywhere, anytime. Try it and see.

BREATHE

Slowing down can be achieved by simply focusing on taking smooth, deliberate, calming breaths. You don't have to be sitting in stillness with your eyes closed, though you can if you want to. Begin by inhaling slowly and mindfully through your nostrils. You might find it useful to count to ten in your head to pace yourself. Pause and hold that breath for just a moment, then breathe out slowly. Try to match the length of your inhale to your exhale, and vice versa. Then do it again.

SCAN YOUR BODY

Focusing on your body can calm and ease your mind. How does your body feel? Notice your feet on the ground, the weight of your torso on your hips and the lengthening of your spine as you sit up straight. If you notice any points of pressure, tension, pain or discomfort in your body, try to relax them. Breathe. Now turn your attention inside. Feel the beat of your heart. Is it fast or slow? How is your stomach feeling? Perhaps it's filled with butterflies, starting to rumble

with hunger or feeling content after a meal. Focusing our attention on the small signals our bodies send us is a great way to check in to see how we're feeling — or if there's anything our bodies have been trying to tell us while we've been too busy to listen.

GROUND YOURSELF

Grounding, also called earthing, is a therapeutic technique that involves doing activities that 'ground' or electrically reconnect you to the earth (for more information, *see* page 182). It can help with healing, pain reduction and mood improvement. If it's safe to do so, remove your shoes and enjoy the feeling of grass, sand or earth pressing up against the soles of your feet. Notice how it feels. Try grounding other parts of your body, too. Touch the grass, sand or earth with your hands and notice the textures and how they feel on your skin. You may feel like walking or touching more slowly or with greater focus — if so, great! You're tuning in and slowing down. Keep following your instincts.

MOVE
YOUR BODY

Modern life has made us increasingly sedentary, with many of us spending our days at desks and our evenings on the couch. But not only are our bodies created to move, movement is the ultimate tonic for our wellbeing and increases our mind-body connection.

Have you noticed that in moments where your body feels sluggish or fatigued, your mind and mood follow suit? When we move, our bodies release chemicals that improve our moods and make us feel more relaxed. Our hearts grow stronger and our circulation improves and beneficially raises our oxygen levels.

Our brains benefit, too. Movement triggers endorphins and the neurotransmitter serotonin, as well as a specific protein called brain-derived neurotrophic factor (BDNF) that protects existing brain cells and promotes new, healthier brain cells, leading to improved brain function. This benefits our mental health in many ways. It enhances our ability to take in new information and retain and recall that information. It also gives us a 'feel-good factor' that helps us go about our daily lives feeling happy and confident. Research shows that walking for just two minutes every hour can offset the health risks of extended periods of sitting, and studies show that exercising in nature boosts the effects.

Experts recommend that most healthy adults get at least 150 minutes of exercise per week. Ideally, you'll spread this exercise out during the course of a week — 30 minutes a day is spot on. You could try brisk walking, biking, swimming, yoga and mowing the lawn, or step it up and do some running, heavy gardening work or dancing. Then there are strength-building exercises, like weight lifting, press-ups and rock climbing.

If a 30-minute burst is too much for you or your schedule, remember that being active for short periods of time throughout the day can add up to provide health benefits, too. And you don't have to deliberately exercise for it to count — incidental activity, such as gardening, housework and getting yourself from place to place without using vehicle transport are also effective ways to get physical.

Here are a few different ways to move your body in everyday life. Mix it up!

- Stand up or walk for all phone and video calls
- Try a standing desk or sit on an exercise ball instead of a chair
- Stretch regularly
- Do gardening work, such as raking, digging, mowing and pruning
- Use alarms or reminders on your phone to remind you to move
- Do calf rises while cleaning your teeth
- Park a couple of blocks away from your destination to increase your walking
- Take a walking meeting
- Skip the lift and take the stairs instead
- Go on a bike ride
- Take your dog, or your neighbour's, for a walk
- Take a yoga or pilates class
- Go on a hike
- Dance

LIVE SIMPLY

Voluntary simplicity is a lifestyle practice that encourages mindfulness and minimalism in the way we design and go about our lives. It's less about deprivation and more about considering your true wants and needs, destressing, decluttering and prioritising non-monetary ways of finding joy and contentment.

Other names this concept goes by include downshifting, minimising, simple living and downscaling. They all allude to a central tenet of stepping back from the hustle and bustle of a life filled with fast-paced work, the pursuit of wealth and recognition, and the stress that often follows. Our modern world's incessant consumption is also taking a huge toll on the environment. City life, in particular, can seem to be all about these things, but it doesn't have to be that way.

A conscious choice to live simply without unnecessary consumption, spending and desires, voluntary simplicity can help free up time and resources to dedicate to family, friends and hobbies instead.

It also helps reduce your carbon footprint (*see* page 76) so you can tread more lightly on the Earth.

A good starting point for some slow but certain changes in the direction of a simpler life is taking a step back and examining all the different aspects of your life. Which ones make you happy and create joy, and which ones drain your energy? What do you truly want in life, and what are the steps you can take to get there? You don't have to spring into action straight away; even simply thinking about how things can be different and setting intentions for the future can be a step towards change.

TAKE STOCK AND DECLUTTER

Think about the material possessions you have amassed in your life. Are they things you want and need, or are you keeping things that no longer serve you? You might have some old picture frames in the cupboard that just need a lick of paint to be as good as new (that you'll probably never get around to fix or hang up) or a stack of well-meant but not-quite-right-for-you gifts that it's time to let go of. By knowing what you have, you'll be able to decide what you no longer need, declutter and be better able to resist the temptation of buying more.

CONSUME CONSCIOUSLY

Conscious consumption, or conscious consumerism, is when a person's buying practices are driven by a commitment to make purchase decisions that have a positive social, economic and environmental impact. In those moments when buying something new is called for, think about how you can do so in the most environmentally or socially responsible way. Need a new bike or jacket? Buy second-hand. Looking for a special gift? Check out a local maker's market or consider making your own — maybe a pinch pot (see page 156) or string bag (see page 168). When shopping for food, reduce your reliance on plastic by visiting stores where you can take your own bags and containers. Reduce food miles by shopping seasonally and locally wherever possible and do all you can to reduce your carbon footprint (see page 76) and impact on the environment. Small actions really add up.

PRIORITISE EXPERIENCES OVER MATERIALISM

Write a list or reflect on the moments in your life where you felt the most joyous or content. There's a good chance you'll focus on special moments with friends and loved ones and time spent in nature or adventuring. Rather than succumbing to the rush of dopamine (feel-good chemicals released as part of the brain's reward system) that often comes with material purchases, try to reconnect and highlight this side of yourself to experience a simpler, more genuine and easier to come by kind of joy.

INCREASE YOUR SELF-SUFFICIENCY

Stepping away from consumerism will, by necessity, mean you must become more self-sufficient. This might mean growing your own vegetables and herbs (see page 68) or riding a bike or walking instead of driving where you need to go. See page 8 for information about the benefits of moving your body.

REFLECT AND REALIGN

As time passes, you might veer off the trail occasionally or find that your needs have changed. Every now and then, it can be helpful to reflect on your progress, review your actions and realign them with your original or new goals. This 'recalibration' will help you keep simplifying your life.

'SIMPLIFY,
SIMPLIFY,
SIMPLIFY'

IN THE EARLY 1850S IN CONCORD, MASSACHUSETTS, AUTHOR AND PHILOSOPHER HENRY DAVID THOREAU WAS ONE OF THE FIRST PEOPLE TO EXPERIMENT WITH LIVING A CONSCIOUSLY SIMPLE LIFE. THOREAU BUILT A SMALL HOUSE ON THE SHORE OF WALDEN POND, WHERE HE LIVED FOR TWO YEARS, DOCUMENTING HIS EXPERIENCE OF VOLUNTARY SIMPLICITY IN HIS FAMOUS WORK, *WALDEN; OR, LIFE IN THE WOODS*. HIS PHILOSOPHY: SIMPLIFY, SIMPLIFY, SIMPLIFY.

TAKE A DIGITAL DETOX

A digital detox – reducing our time on the various devices that connect us to digital technology, like phones, tablets and laptops – can improve our mental and physical health and help us become more present in the world around us.

Some of the benefits of taking a break from digital devices include better posture and sleep, greater alignment with our circadian rhythm (*see* page 18), reduced anxiety, greater productivity and deeper, more connected friendships. A digital detox gives our busy, often overstimulated brains a chance to rest and daydream, and it helps us become more grounded, attentive and present. It won't be easy to begin with, but it will get easier. Here are some tips for getting started.

START SMALL

When we rely so heavily on something, going cold turkey can be daunting. So, let's start small. How long can you comfortably go without your digital devices? At what point does the absence become uncomfortable? Five minutes? An hour? A day? Set an intention to spend a manageable amount of time away from your devices — and then grow it. Planning ahead will help you step away. Pop out for a walk or to do some errands and leave your phone at home. Disconnecting can be wonderfully freeing, and there's a good chance you'll realise you didn't really need it with you at all.

EMBRACE BOREDOM

Our devices provide us with a dopamine hit (a rush of feel-good chemicals released by the brain's reward system) whenever we engage with them, and our dopamine-hungry brains drive us to pick them up at the slightest hint of boredom or restlessness. But boredom is a wonderful thing. The breeding ground for creativity and exploration, it's a space for discovery, play and invention. When we take a digital detox, we're gifting our mind the opportunity to make its own discoveries. How wonderful!

NOTICE THE BENEFITS

Detoxing from your devices will be an adjustment for your mind and body. Take some time to notice and appreciate how you feel when you're not distracted by digital technology. What did you do instead? Maybe you went for a walk, did some gardening or returned to an unfinished project. You might even have started a new one. Over time you'll notice you're sleeping better, feeling more grounded in your surroundings and feeling more connected to the people around you.

BRING IT INTO YOUR EVERYDAY

Feel the benefits of your digital detox by intentionally bringing elements of it into your everyday. Schedule 'Do Not Disturb' on your phone, which turns off notifications for parts of the day, and set boundaries for yourself with an allocated daily window (or windows) for social media. If that's too hard, try setting app limits that control how long you can scroll or download apps that limit or restrict your time on social media. Turn off notifications on every app except your essentials, and watch as your devices, and your mind, quieten down.

ALIGN YOUR CIRCADIAN RHYTHM

The circadian rhythm is an internal body clock that constantly cycles between alertness and sleepiness. Sometimes called the sleep-wake cycle, adhering to yours is the key to quality sleep and will put you more in sync with your wild self.

Almost all living organisms' patterns of waking and resting are governed by circadian rhythms, which are in turn aligned with nature. A vital system that evolved over three billion years ago, our circadian rhythm helps keep our bodies healthy. It developed in cyanobacteria, a blue-green algae that scientists believe evolved to align with light and dark. For these algae, the day became a time to photosynthesise and grow, and the night a time to rest and generate more energy.

In humans, darkness prompts the pineal gland to start producing an important sleep hormone called melatonin; light causes that production to stop. Melatonin helps regulate circadian rhythm and synchronise our sleep-wake cycle with night and day.

When we override our body's natural rhythm and decrease melatonin production, we can fall into chronic sleep deprivation, which can lead to serious health impacts like heart disease, diabetes and depression.

Many aspects of our modern lives are not in sync with our circadian rhythm. Jet lag — that groggy, intensely fatigued feeling that comes when you fly across three or more time zones and land in misalignment with your body's internal clock — is perhaps the most extreme example. But other, more ordinary aspects of our day-to-day lives, such as staying up late to work or socialise or spending time on screens, are also examples of how we're unintentionally disrupting ourselves.

Before electricity, our ancestors honoured the energetic waxing and waning of day and night, and they lived in alignment with their circadian rhythms. Want to feel more rested? Try tuning into yours.

START LIGHT

Light is the ultimate boost to kick-start your day; exposing our eyes and brain to light supports us in feeling awake and alert. Start your day by enjoying the morning light — open your curtains, drink your morning coffee outdoors or take a walk before diving into the day's tasks. Your mind and body will feel the benefits of waking up with natural light.

REPLACE CATNAPPING AND CAFFEINE WITH GENTLE MOVEMENT

We often experience an energy slump in the afternoon, and it can be tempting to snooze or drink coffee or black tea (which has half the caffeine of coffee) to overcome this sense of inertia. Instead of catnapping or hitting the sugar or caffeine during this time — which can make it harder to sleep at night, as it takes four to six hours to exit your system — try gently moving your body instead (*see* page 8).

CUT OUT THE EVENING SCREEN TIME

Screen time is recognised as one of the most disruptive presences in our lives (*see* page 16), and it heavily impacts our circadian rhythm. Just like the sunlight in the morning, the blue light from screens and electronic devices is stimulating to our brains and slows the release of melatonin, meaning our sleep suffers. In the two hours leading up to your desired bedtime, put away your devices, turn down your lights and invite your body clock to wind down to prepare for a good night's sleep.

CONSISTENCY IS KEY

Establishing a regular sleep pattern that honours the circadian rhythm is the key to a good sleep. Melatonin triggers sleepiness in the body around 9pm and eases around 7.30am. A consistent sleep pattern will help train and maintain your circadian rhythm, helping to avoid night waking and gifting you the kind of deep, restorative sleep your mind and body need to be at their best.

FOLLOW
THE
SEASONS

As our Earth makes its annual revolution around the sun,
our environment transforms and experiences a cycle of rest,
rising, growth and rejuvenation. By observing and celebrating
its procession through spring, summer, autumn (fall) and winter,
we increase our connection to nature and all its beauty.

There's a natural rhythm and order to the seasons. Many contemporary and ancient indigenous cultures live in symbiosis with them, marking their progress with rituals to welcome and celebrate the unfurling and new growth of spring, the plentiful heat of summer, the poignant decline of autumn and the cold starkness of winter. They know when to plant and how to nurture and grow. They know when and where to forage and how to preserve and store their excess food supplies to survive the cold months or monsoons.

Bird, animal and plant species' life cycles are also governed by the seasons. Hedgehogs, bears and snakes enter long periods of hibernation in the colder months before emerging to thrive in spring and summer. Birds nest and breed in spring ahead of hatching their eggs and nurturing their young in summer and autumn. Deciduous trees shed their leaves in autumn to conserve energy through the cold of winter, then blossom in spring and grow in summer. Seeds sprout from the ground in spring, reaching for the warmth of the sun.

The conveniences of twenty-first century living invite us to resist seasonal change. Electricity means we can light and heat or cool our homes to a consistent glow and temperature. The modern food industry allows fruits and vegetables to be produced all year round and transported around the globe — many are picked when unripe to sustain them during transport and then artificially ripened with the use of chemicals before they are sold, which is not only bad news for your health but also for the nutritional value of the foods.

For many of us living in urban environments, our daily schedules don't change, even when the seasons do. Embracing and following the seasons enables us to live more in tune with nature and helps protect our environment by working with, rather than against it. Here are some simple ways to welcome and make the most of every time of year.

SPRING

Springtime begins when the sun crosses the celestial equator and moves into the hemisphere you're in. If you're living in the Northern Hemisphere of the globe, it's when the sun crosses from south to north, and vice versa for those living in the Southern Hemisphere. On this date, called the equinox, day and night are of equal length. As spring progresses, the days become longer. Seeds sprout, blossoms emerge and baby birds and animals are born. Go on a hike or a micro-adventure (*see* pages 110, 100) or go wildlife spotting (*see* page 128), and notice how everything seems to spring back to life. Plant spring seeds like beans, carrot and cucumber in your garden.

SUMMER

The warm, sunny and light summer months draw us outside. We're drawn to swim at the beach (*see* page 176) or pool, soak up vitamin D from the sun, walk and play in the park, and camp and ramble in nature (*see* page 118). The summer solstice marks the longest, lightest day of the year and is when Earth's North Pole has its maximum tilt towards the sun. In many cultures around the world, it's celebrated with music, feasting and time outdoors. Celebrate its abundance by making flower and greenery crowns and enjoying a seasonal picnic with your favourite people.

AUTUMN (FALL)

Like spring, autumn is a season of transition. It begins with the autumn equinox, when night and day are the same length. For those living in the Northern Hemisphere, this is when the sun crosses the celestial equator and moves into the Southern Hemisphere, and vice versa for those living in the Southern Hemisphere. As autumn progresses, the sun rises later and sets earlier, the leaves on deciduous trees turn a stunning palette of orange, red and brown before they fall and our bodies begin to slow down. This is the season to walk in the forest and forage for mushrooms (*see* page 136) and make jams and preserves.

WINTER

As the shortest and darkest day of the year falls upon us at the winter solstice, embrace cosiness with the Danish and Norwegian concept of hygge (hoo-ga). This concept is all about cosiness, relaxation and comfort, and doing the things that make you happy. It's about being present in the moment and indulging in pleasures, which may explain why the average Dane eats 12.3 kg of candy a year — more than any other country in the world. You can hygge with your friends or you can hygge alone; the main thing is creating an atmosphere of cosiness and comfort to relax in. Read a book under a soft blanket, light candles and make nourishing soups and stews, or bake a cake and share it around. Watching a sports match on TV with a group of friends is also a prime breeding ground for hygge. To mark the winter solstice, the shortest day of the year, build a bonfire to gather around with friends and family to light up the dark and celebrate that the light is coming back.

25

SEASONAL EATING

In the wild, the fruits and vegetables we eat grow seasonally. When we eat seasonally, we choose fruits and vegetables that are naturally ready for harvest at that time. We're also more likely to buy food that is grown locally, reducing food miles (the distance food has travelled from its source) and the resulting environmental impacts. Seasonal produce is generally fresher, more nutritious, tastier, and it's easier on your pocket, too.

Some ways to eat seasonally include visiting farmers' markets, choosing organic produce and growing your own vegetables. When you eat produce that is in season, you'll notice they're more flavoursome than their non-seasonal counterparts. Here are some of the most recognisable seasonal fruits and vegetables.

FOLLOW THE SEASONS

SPRING

ASPARAGUS, BLUEBERRIES, CHERRIES,
MANGOES, PEAS, SPRING ONIONS

SUMMER

APRICOTS, AVOCADOS, BANANAS, CAPSICUMS,
CORN, CUCUMBERS, EGGPLANTS, FIGS,
KIWIFRUITS, NECTARINES, PASSIONFRUITS,
RASPBERRIES, STRAWBERRIES, TOMATOES,
WATERMELONS

AUTUMN (FALL)

APPLES, BROCCOLI, CARROTS, GRAPES,
LETTUCE, MANDARINS, MUSHROOMS,
SPINACH, SWEET POTATOES

WINTER

BEETROOT, BRUSSELS SPROUTS, CABBAGE,
CELERY, CUSTARD APPLE, KALE,
LEMONS, LIMES, RHUBARB

READ
THE MOON

Almost every night, and sometimes in the daytime too, we can see
the moon in the sky. Like everything in nature, the moon is always
changing, shifting through eight distinct lunar phases every month
(roughly). Learning to recognise these phases is an ancient
and effective way to mark the passing of time.

The moon is a cold, dry orb covered with craters, rocks and dust, and its gravitational pull creates and controls Earth's ocean tides (for more information on the tides, *see* page 188). A lunar phase is the name for one of eight distinct shapes the moon moves through across the course of a lunar month — a cycle that lasts 29.5 days, which is about the length of time it takes for the moon to orbit the Earth.

Of course, it's not really the moon that is changing shape; it's our earthly perspective of the moon, which depends on how much sunlight is beaming onto the moon's day side, or illuminated side, at any given time (the opposite is its night or shadow side — the side we can't see from Earth). At the beginning of each cycle, the earth sits between the moon and the sun, blocking the light necessary to make the moon visible.

THE MOON, NATURE AND US

The moon's effect has been observed in organisms like ocean corals, which time their spawning based on the lunar cycle. It's essential to the migration and navigation of birds and drives ocean tides, generating tidal force with its gravitational pull. The tidal force causes Earth's waters to bulge out on the side closest to the moon and the side farthest from the moon. These bulges of water are what we call high tides.

Many people are affected by the moon and its phases, too. Restless sleeps, 'lunacy' (intermittent insanity once believed to be related to phases of the moon) and menstrual cycles that sync up with its cycle all feature strongly in our cultural history. Theories of lunacy have been discounted multiple times, but research from 2013 found that people stay up later and sleep less before the full moon and do the opposite before the new moon. Some researchers believe there's a connection between lunar cycles and women's menstrual cycles, too, with one positing that in ancient times, human reproductive behaviour was synchronous with the moon, but that our modern lifestyle, notably our increased exposure to artificial light, has changed this relationship.

Then there's permaculture, an agricultural system that focuses on self-sufficiency and sustainable ways. Permaculture draws inspiration from nature to develop synergetic farming systems based on crop diversity, resilience, natural productivity and sustainability. 'Moon planting' is one of the principles of permaculture. It holds that while the moon is waxing, a plant's sap flow is drawn up, and that this is the best time for sowing and transplanting flowering annuals, biennials, grains and melons. On the flipside, when the moon is waning, the sap flow is drawn down. This pulls energy to the plants' roots, which is more suited to planting root crops and perennials.

If you choose to learn to read the moon for yourself, see if you can find a connection between its phases and your mood, monthly flow or energy levels. Once you have learned to read the moon, you might like to note how you respond to its different phases in your nature journal (*see* page 82). Over time you might start to spot or recognise patterns in your energy or mood throughout the lunar phases and will be able to draw your own conclusions.

01 NEW MOON

The lunar cycle begins with a new moon, one that is almost invisible to the eye. A new moon will likely be the one night of the month where there's no moonlight in the night sky.

02 WAXING CRESCENT

The term 'waxing' describes the moon when its illuminated area is increasing. You see a thin but growing fraction of its day side increasing from right to left if you're in the Northern Hemisphere, and from left to right in the Southern Hemisphere.

03 FIRST QUARTER

A week after the new moon, the moon enters the first quarter of the cycle and is halfway to becoming a full moon. During the first quarter, almost half of the moon will be visible from Earth.

04 WAXING GIBBOUS

As the moon continues to wax, or grow, towards a full moon, it enters its gibbous phase. It looks more than half lit, but less than full.

05   FULL MOON

Approximately two weeks after the
new moon, the moon moves out of the
Earth's shadow and becomes entirely
illuminated, appearing full.

06   WANING GIBBOUS

'Waning' comes from the Old English word
'wonian', meaning to lessen or diminish.
As the moon wanes, you'll notice its
illuminated side is the reverse of when
it was waxing. If you're in the Northern
Hemisphere it diminishes from left to
right; in the Southern Hemisphere, this
movement occurs from right to left.

07   THIRD QUARTER

As the moon continues to wane, it reaches
its third quarter. Again, almost half of the
moon is visible, but this time on the reverse
side of when it was waxing.

08   WANING CRESCENT

As the moon disappears back into the
shadow cast by the Earth, it wanes
to a thin crescent.

HOME LIFE

APPLY
BIOPHILIC
DESIGN

Biophilic design is an architectural and interior design movement that aims to integrate nature into our homes and workspaces. It's founded on the notion that the more our built environment reflects and is connected to nature, the more our health and wellbeing benefit.

Biophilia is derived from the Greek words for 'life' and 'love', literally translating as 'love of life'. The theory was developed by psychoanalyst Erich Fromm in 1973 to describe 'the passionate love of life and of all that is alive', and hypothesises that humans have an innate instinct to seek connection with nature and other forms of life and living beings.

Our modern lives see us spending an increased amount of time indoors, with the average American spending 90% of their time inside. But research shows that exposure to greenery and natural spaces does wonders for our physical and mental health — from relaxing our nervous system and supporting our digestion to restoring our energy and lowering our heart rate and blood pressure. Applying biophilic design principles to our homes and workspaces by bringing the outside in is a great way to gain the benefits of nature and greenery.

Biophilic design's genesis in architecture and interiors can be traced to the early years of the 21st century. Architect Frank Lloyd Wright's organic architecture is a famous example. In his work, curving architectural forms flow into dense landscapes of trees, boulders and even waterfalls. Cantilever roofs extend almost impossibly outwards and floor-to-ceiling windows invite the outside in. His most renowned work is arguably Fallingwater, which was built partly over a waterfall in the Laurel Highlands of southwest Pennsylvania in 1939.

But of course, the concepts and principles of biophilic design go much further back. Many indigenous design traditions, such as Japanese zen (which focuses on simplicity, enclosure and completeness), shou sugi ban (a wood charring technique) and wabi-sabi (which emphasises simplicity, tranquillity and naturalness), have long sought to place nature at the centre of the human experience.

Happily, it's possible to harness the benefits of biophilic design without having to commission a world-famous architect, whether you live in an inner-city apartment, share house or suburban family home. Inviting nature in is as simple as utilising natural materials, patterns, textures and colours in our spaces.

GREEN YOUR SPACE

The colour green is a calming tonic for the human brain. Introduce shades of green to your space with paints and furnishings, or learn to cultivate and grow indoor plants (*see* page 42), which aid wellbeing by helping to keep the air fresh and clean. They can also boost your immune system, increase productivity, help with allergies and even help you sleep better. A living wall is an especially luscious way to bring the outside in.

CREATE A LIVING WALL

Living walls are walls of plants grown vertically in a shelf-like structure. Sometimes also called green walls, vertical gardens or plant walls, they're a good fit in narrow or constrained urban spaces, like apartments and balconies. They can even be used as room dividers. Commercially made living walls often comprise modular systems fixed to a wall or special shelves with frames for plant pots or narrow beds, but it's quite possible to create your own from a regular bookshelf or timber offcuts.

A BREATH OF FRESH AIR

When we're indoors, windows are our ultimate gateway to nature. Opening a window invites fresh air in, which helps rid the home of toxins and allergens and lets us feel the warmth or cool of the outside world. We can hear the rain fall, the wind blow and the birds sing. Aim to open your windows for at least five minutes — ideally 20 minutes — every day.

LET THERE BE LIGHT

Letting in the light can help blur the boundary between inside and out. Natural light influences our circadian rhythm and sleep cycles (*see* page 18) and our overall wellbeing, so let as much natural light into your space as you can. Clean your windows of dirt and grime and open the curtains and blinds. Arrange your furniture to make the most of the natural light throughout the day.

SURROUND YOURSELF WITH NATURE'S BEAUTY

Natural materials, patterns, colours and shapes in our spaces represent the presence of nature and the outdoors. Choose wood over plastic and organic curves over straight lines when selecting furniture and decor, and clad your walls in natural fibres and timbers. Landscape paintings or photographs, floral arrangements (*see* page 60) and earthenware and ceramics will all help cocoon your space in nature too.

CULTIVATE INDOOR PLANTS

Plants are incredibly beneficial to our mental and physical wellbeing. They help keep our air fresh and clean by eliminating harmful toxins. Their lush greenery has calming qualities and gives our indoor spaces a touch of colour.

Plants do the opposite of what we humans do when we breathe. Put simply, they release oxygen and absorb carbon dioxide, thereby cleaning the air. Research by National Aeronautics and Space Administration (NASA) found that in just 24 hours some houseplants can remove up to 87 per cent of air toxins.

Some plants are quite delicate and need a lot of care, while others are very hardy and don't need much attention. Take care to choose plants that work in your space — and that work for you.

PLANT CARE

To get plants to thrive indoors, it's important to emulate their natural environment as best as you can.

LIGHT

All plants require light to live, but different plants enjoy different levels of light, from basking in full sun to low, indirect light. Plants like ZZ plant, peace lilies and other dark-leaved plants that, in the wild, would grow in shaded places like the forest floor prefer indirect light, and some will even tolerate low-light conditions.

SOIL

Plants have different preferences and needs when it comes to potting mix. Succulents and cacti, for example, love a sandy, fast-drying mix, while many jungle species prefer moisture-retaining soil (and a humid environment). Most plants thrive in well-draining soil, which is what you get when you buy a standard premium potting mix. You can often find potting mix that's specifically created for certain plant types, such as orchid or succulent mix. You can also make your own by adding horticultural charcoal, perlite and peat moss (also called coir peat) to standard premium potting mix to improve it's water-retaining and draining properties.

WATER

Overwatering is one of the most common reasons houseplants die, so it's important to get to know your plants and their varying needs. Check to see if the soil is wet or dry before watering by inserting a fingertip into the top inch of soil. If it's dry, it's safe to water; if it's wet, leave it for a few days then check again. You can expect to need to water your plants more often in warm weather and if they are in a spot with brighter light, and less in cold weather and lower light conditions.

If you're new to plant care, aim to adopt plants that are easy to care for and difficult to kill! Succulents and cacti are a great example of low-maintenance plant friends; they don't need much watering, can handle neglect and love warm and sunny spots.

Here are some luscious and sturdy plants to start greening your space with. Many are also easy to propagate (*see* page 46), making them the perfect choice if you want to cheaply grow and expand your collection.

ALOE VERA
Aloe barbadensis miller

Aloe vera is a succulent that loves to bask in the sun all day and will thrive on any bright windowsill or sunny spot in your home. Water sparingly.

ZZ PLANT
Zamioculcas zamiifolia

This tropical perennial grows smooth, naturally shiny leaves that range from bright lime to emerald shades of green, depending on the plant's maturity. It's an easy-care houseplant thanks to its tolerance of low light and low water requirements.

DEVIL'S IVY
Epipremnum aureum

Commonly known as pothos, this hardy vine is called devil's ivy for a reason; it can withstand and grow in almost all conditions. There are many types of devil's ivy, and their leaves range in colour from dark green to speckled to almost completely white — pick a variety with lots of green in the leaves if you want an easy-care plant. This one is perfect for propagating and dispersing into other pots.

ASPARAGUS FERN
Asparagus setaceus

Despite its name, this plant isn't a real fern and is far less needy and specific than members of the fern family. Provided the soil it's in remains moist, it will adapt to both sunny spots or low light.

44

RUBBER PLANT
Ficus elastica

The rubber plant is adaptive to low light and only requires water once the top inch of soil has dried out. The rubber plant is also great at filtering chemicals from the air, making it a great plant for city dwellers.

SPIDER PLANT
Chlorophytum comosum

Known for their small, spidery offshoots that make for easy repotting, spider plants like a well-lit spot and a weekly watering. They're very efficient carbon-monoxide absorbers, making them great for purifying urban spaces.

SWISS CHEESE PLANT
Monstera deliciosa

While there are many types of monstera, *Monstera deliciosa*, commonly know as Swiss cheese plant, is a firm favourite with plant lovers everywhere. They appreciate a warm, humid environment, medium to bright indirect light and like to dry out a little between drinks. Rotate yours periodically to ensure even growth on all sides. If your space is too small for the majestic deliciosa, opt for an *adansonii* (mini Swiss cheese plant) instead.

SNAKE PLANT
Dracaena trifasciata

Snake plants are hard to kill, surviving up to a month without water in almost any indoor environment. Even better, snake plants are known for their air-purifying qualities.

PROPAGATE PLANTS

Propagation is the process of creating new plants
from seeds, cuttings, roots or bulbs. For established plants that
are capable of propagation, it's a fantastic way to spread foliage
across multiple pots and grow your indoor plant collection.

GATHER

SCISSORS OR PRUNING SHEARS

SMALL GLASS CONTAINERS

WATER

SPHAGNUM MOSS

A PLANT TO TAKE CUTTING FROM

SMALL PLASTIC PLANTER POT

GOOD QUALITY POTTING MIX

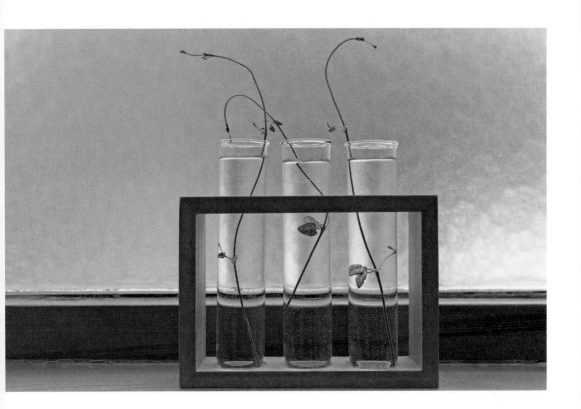

FIND THE RIGHT PLANT

Not all plants are easy to propagate, so if you're a beginner, take cuttings or new growth from a robust plant that will be easy to grow. Some of the best plants for propagating include:

- Devil's ivy, also known as pothos (*Epipremnum*)
- Chinese money plant (*Pilea peperomioides*)
- Spider plant (*Chlorophytum comosum*)
- Snake plant (*Dracaena trifasciata*)
- Swiss cheese plant (*Monstera deliciosa* and *Monstera adansonii*)

TAKE YOUR CUTTINGS

Different types of plants require different propagation methods, so start by determining how to best propagate your plant.

Stem cuttings — many plants, such as trailing and creeping plants, like devil's ivy and Swiss cheese plants, are propagated using stem cuttings. Use clean pruning shears to cut a finger's width below a root node.

Plantlets and offsets — some plants grow mini baby versions (plantlets and offsets) of themselves, including Chinese money plants and spider plants. For spider plants, simply cut the dangling offsets off at the aerial stem. For plantlets, where the plant

Don't be disheartened if your cutting isn't successful — this is normal so just try again. If you want to increase your chances of success, you can dip the cutting in rooting hormone before adding it to water or sphagnum.

CRAFT YOUR PROPAGATION DESIGN

There are lots of crafty and decorative ways to display your propagating plants (especially if you're rooting them in water) to provide your space with some natural design features (see page 38). Glass is translucent, lending itself to display — in jars on windowsills, in test tubes in racks or in simple holders, or even in a champagne flute! You'll be pleased when you see the roots emerge but don't rush right into planting — the roots need to be long and strong before the plant is ready to be planted.

PLANTING INTO SOIL

When your propagations have 7–10cm (3–5in) of roots, they are ready to be planted into potting mix. It can take a few weeks or even months before your cuttings are ready, depending on the season and which propagation technique you use, so be patient and enjoy the process. When ready, fill a plastic planter pot in a suitable size for your cutting about two-thirds of the way with a good-quality premium potting mix or propagation mix. Carefully place the rooted plant in the middle and fill up the pot with more potting mix. Lastly, water the plant to let the roots and soil settle in, letting excess water drain off. Your new plant is now ready for a decorative pot and a place to brighten up your home.

grows side shoots at the base, wait for the mini plant to grow big enough to develop a root network, then use a sharp knife or secateurs to separate it from the mother plant at the roots.

GROW ROOTS

As with any plant, your propagations need to be nurtured so they can grow. There are some plant cuttings, like aloe vera, that will grow by just adding it to a pot of soil, but most will require a network of roots before they are planted to be successful. You can grow roots by simply placing the cutting in a small glass container filled with water and changing the water every few days. You can also use sphagnum moss, which creates the dark, moist environment roots naturally thrive in for a much faster result — albeit perhaps not as visually pleasant. Wet the sphagnum so it expands in size and wrap it around the base of the cutting. Place the wrapped cutting in your container and fill it with more moss. Take care to keep it moist (but not wet). Watch your cuttings or plantlets for signs of root growth. Make sure you give your propagations plenty of natural light and be patient with them as they take root.

REWILD YOUR GARDEN

Rewilding is the act of restoring an area of land to its natural, uncultivated state (*see* page IX for more information). It can happen anywhere — even in your backyard. With a bit of planning, love and attention, the dullest and least abundant of outdoor spaces can be nurtured back into a flourishing state.

We don't all have access to expansive landscapes or the power to reclaim large buildings to convert into green spaces. So how can we bring the philosophy — and practice — of rewilding into our own lives? If you have even the smallest of outdoor spaces, from a backyard to a window box, there are ways you can contribute to the rewilding of our world.

All types of rewilding share several key principles, no matter what the location or scale of the rewilding project. Keeping them in mind will help you take pride and joy in what you're able to achieve. Firstly, embrace natural processes. Secondly, encourage biodiversity so all living things — plants, animals and microorganisms — can thrive. Thirdly, enjoy being more hands off than a traditional or managed garden might demand of you — rewilding requires you to let nature lead. After establishing your space and introducing your plants, let it run wild and notice how the plants, soil, insects and birds start to thrive and benefit from your little patch of wilderness — along with your mental, physical and emotional wellbeing.

SPOT WHAT'S THRIVING

The ultimate way to determine what will grow well in your outdoor space is to notice which of the plants are thriving in your neighbourhood. Can you spot any edibles or flowering beauties on your walks that you'd like to include in your rewilding project? Is there a native plant that is flourishing in your street? Perhaps a type of grass or groundcover that just loves to grow? Take care to learn about any invasive species you should avoid. Discovering which plants are naturally thriving in your local area will help you introduce species that should thrive under your love and care, too.

AVOID PESTICIDES

You want to avoid the use of any harsh chemicals in your natural space. Pesticides and non-organic fertilisers contain chemicals that kill insects and damage the integrity of the soil. If you want to rewild your green space, you'll need to enable it to thrive as naturally as possible. Instead, rely on compost (see page 53) and natural fertilisers to nourish your garden.

MAKE USE OF VINES

If you have a bare wall or roof space, make use of vines to climb and give your vertical spaces a green boost. This tip is particularly great for homes with small, walled balconies and courtyards, as so many inner-city apartments and houses have. Use trellises and wooden ladders to support and train the vines to climb — some vines will even just climb on their own. Figure out which vines will thrive in your area and enjoy looking out at a green wall. A living wall (see page 40) is another creative way to maximise luscious green leaves in your space.

CREATE GARDEN CORRIDORS

Connecting different habitats is an important part of the rewilding ethos. Birds can fly from one isolated habitat to another, but ground-dwelling animals don't have the same luxury and face plenty of obstacles and unnatural dangers when they move from one habitat to another. Digging holes under fences or even cutting away sections of wood (with your neighbour's blessing, of course) is a great way to assist creatures in moving from your garden to your neighbour's. It can also help you spread the rewilding message — who knows, you might inspire your neighbour to rewild their outdoor space, too.

CREATE AN ANIMAL-FRIENDLY OASIS

A bug hotel (*see* page 64) will attract and welcome insects to your space, but there are other oases we can provide for wildlife. In autumn and winter, leave the leaves that fall to the ground, as many bugs rely on them for food and shelter in the cold months. You don't have to leave them where they fall; you can collect them and move them to a part of your garden where they're out of the way. A log or rock pile will also invite exploration by bugs and other creatures. A bird bath gives birds a place to drink and bathe, especially in the warmer months. You could use an overturned lid, a dish or purchase a purpose-made bath — just take care to elevate it so the birds can drink safely. You can also introduce bird feeders with a variety of seeds. Enjoy the sights and sounds of our avian friends as they feed, drink and bathe.

CREATE A COMPOST PILE

There's no such thing as waste in nature. A compost pile is the ultimate way to fertilise your garden, keep your home's waste out of landfill and live more simply (*see* page 10). There are many types of compost bins on the market, but you can also use a tub or wooden crate that has been dug into the soil. A compost pile needs to be a certain size to do its thing, so it's best to get a large container — it's called a pile for a reason.

When creating a compost pile, it's important to make sure you've got the right ratio between brown and green matter. Brown matter (carbon) is dry and usually brown stuff, such as dead leaves, small twigs, straw, pine needles, hay and shredded paper and cardboard. Green matter (nitrogen), which may or may not be green, includes all wet and fresh materials, such as kitchen waste, grass clippings and plant prunings.

A good balance is a ratio of about 4:1 brown to green matter, but anywhere between 1:1 and 10:1 will work — the important thing is to make sure there's more brown matter than green, or the heaps will start to smell and attract pests.

Keep a small, lidded container in your kitchen and place food scraps in there — all except for meat and dairy, as they harbour some unhealthy bacteria and can attract unwanted animal attention. When the kitchen container is full, empty it into the compost. Frequently turn your compost with a garden fork to aerate and mix it, and take finished compost from the bottom of the heap to add to your garden. Then watch your garden flourish with the power of your own organic waste!

GROW A WILDFLOWER MEADOW

Wildflowers are flowering plants that grow without human aid.
We tend to think of the flowers that bloom along country
roadsides and in woodlands, forests, prairies and mountains as
wildflowers, but they can — and do — grow in cities, too.
You can even grow them in your front yard.

In recent years, keen rewilders and environmentalists have rallied against the perfection of perfectly manicured lawns and begun planting wildflower meadows in their place instead, as they aid biodiversity and help foster a robust ecosystem. A wildflower meadow brings a visually pleasing abundance of colour to your garden and neighbourhood, but more importantly, it will bring valuable pollinators (*see* page 64), as birds, beetles, bees and butterflies are attracted to a diversity of colour when foraging.

Replacing lawn with native wildflowers is a shift from high-maintenance to low-maintenance garden care, too. Wildflowers require little work, are relatively drought tolerant and will need far less watering than a lawn — an enticing feature as our climate crisis becomes more present. Planting native perennials (plants that live for many years) also means your meadow will flower year after year.

PREPARE THE SITE OF YOUR MEADOW

In the months leading up to planting, place a large tarp over the area that will become your meadow and secure it down with rocks or bricks. This will deprive any grass or other undesirable growth of sunlight. Eventually they will die off, and you'll be able to take the next step in preparing your meadow.

CULTIVATE YOUR BED

If remnants of grass or other plants remain in your meadow's bed, place sheets of old cardboard over the soil to block the light and slow their growth. Eventually, it will break down and add a layer of nutritious carbon to the soil, but don't wait for that to happen. As soon as your cardboard is in place, add a thick layer of fresh soil and compost over the top.

SOW YOUR SEEDS

Most plant nurseries and garden centres stock wildflower seeds, seedlings and even established plants. You can also buy seeds online or from seed-saving and seed-swapping groups. Wildflowers that are native to where you live will do especially well, so source those wherever possible. If you're working with seeds, mix them together in a bowl, then evenly toss handfuls over the soil, making sure not to neglect any areas. Gently pat the seeds down with a rake or your hands, taking care not to push the seeds too deep into the soil, as many wildflowers thrive on the surface of the soil. A general rule of thumb when sowing seeds is to plant them at a depth that is twice the diameter of the seed. Aim to sow your wildflower seeds in autumn so they are ready to bloom in spring.

BE PATIENT

As with most gardening projects, we must practise delayed gratification. After planting in autumn, the seeds will enjoy a damp, dark winter before germinating, sprouting and eventually budding and flowering into full bloom in spring and summer. Enjoy welcoming in the warmer months with your wildflower meadow.

NO GARDEN? NO PROBLEM!

You don't need a garden to enjoy wildflowers. Many gardening centres now sell window-box gardens for indoor and outdoor use. If you're handy, you could make your own. Starting a garden from scratch also means you can enjoy planting your meadow in a weed-free environment. Fill your garden box with high-quality potting mix and compost (*see* page 53 to learn how to make your own compost pile) before planting your wildflower seeds. In some places you're allowed to plant on the nature strip in front of your house, but check with your local council before doing so to make sure it's allowed and if there are any rules you need to follow.

CREATE IKEBANA WILDFLOWER ARRANGEMENTS

Flowers are symbols of love, hope, connection
and community. Throughout history we have cultivated,
harvested and foraged them to celebrate and communicate.
Bring wildflowers into your home with the Japanese
art of mindful flower arranging: ikebana.

GATHER

A SHALLOW VASE

WATER

PRUNING SHEARS

A SPIKY FLOWER FROG

FLOWERS

We move fast in the modern world, often buying flowers on the go to decorate our spaces or celebrate a loved one. Convenience stores stock intentionally themed bouquets, while florists have perfectly crafted bunches we can grab. Instead of consuming, let's bring the acts of mindfulness into our flower decorations and arrange our own.

Ikebana is the Japanese art of flower arranging. It is over 1,000 years old and is still a widely practised and highly respected cultural art form in modern-day Japan. Loosely, ikebana translates to 'making flowers come alive'. Different types of flowers can be used, and an arrangement's aim is to evoke emotion in the observer. As with many Japanese cultural practices, ikebana emphasises intuition, focus and mindfulness.

The four principles of ikebana are a fresh approach, movement, balance and harmony, and the three elements are line, colour and mass. It can help to think of an ikebana arrangement as a floral sculpture where all of these principles are in play. No two arrangements will be the same.

Rather than stuffing a bouquet with as many flowers as possible, aim to intentionally select and style your flower arrangement. With an ikebana arrangement, being as thoughtful and mindful as you can when arranging the flowers is key. You can use flowers that you pick from your own wildflower meadow (*see* page 54), garden or neighbourhood, or select single-stem flowers and greenery from a local florist.

COLLECT AND GATHER

Choose flowers and greenery that you are drawn to; they can be a variety of colours and shapes. In the practice of ikebana, stems of different lengths are chosen to represent heaven (the tallest), earth (the second tallest) and humankind (the third tallest). You don't need many stems to include in your arrangement, between 5 and 13 is plenty.

FASTEN YOUR STEMS

Place your flower frog inside your shallow vase. It will be the base in which you stabilise your ikebana arrangement. Then, use your pruning shears to trim your stems to their desired lengths and place them in the flower frog at your desired angles. When curating your arrangement, arrange and place your stems according to the four principles and the three elements in a way that prioritises simplicity, structure and beauty and feels right to you.

CURATE YOUR ARRANGEMENT

Work your way through your collected flowers and greenery and experiment with different combinations. Try arranging by colour, shape or size until you create something that is especially pleasing — bearing in mind the four principles and the three elements. Ultimately, it's about mindfulness and intentionally creating an arrangement that brings you joy.

CELEBRATE

Your ikebana arrangement can be for a loved one or kept entirely for you to enjoy in your home space. Find a place to showcase your creation, making sure it's got enough light and water to stay fresh in the days to come. Freshening up the water every day or two will help it last longer.

BUILD A BUG HOTEL

From butterflies and beetles to spiders and bees, bugs are vital to the survival of our ecosystems. They aerate the soil, pollinate blossoms and control plant pests. With a custom-made bug hotel, you can welcome these humble creatures into your garden.

GATHER

REPURPOSED, UNTREATED
TIMBER TO ACT AS A FRAME

INTERIOR ITEMS, SUCH AS BAMBOO POLES,
DRY LEAVES, BARK AND CARDBOARD ROLLS

THIN ROPE

SCISSORS

A HAND DRILL OR ELECTRIC DRILL

DRILL BIT SLIGHTLY WIDER
THAN YOUR ROPE

HAMMER

NAILS

Insects are crucial components of our ecosystems, where they perform many important functions. Beetles, for example, are scavengers, feeding on dead animals and fallen trees and recycling nutrients back into the soil. Pollinators, such as bees, move pollen from flower to flower when they land on them, which pollinates the plants and enables them to reproduce.

Albert Einstein once said, 'Mankind will not survive the honeybees' disappearance for more than five years.' He was right — the survival of our planet rests on the shoulders of bees. Without bees, our natural ecosystem would cease to exist.

Sitting low to the bottom of the food chain, insects and other bugs support biodiversity as they are an important source of energy for other species, but they also support our soil health and pollinate the plants that grow the fruits and vegetables we rely on for food. But in recent years, scientists have revealed that insect populations are declining around the world due to habitat loss, the heavy use of toxic pesticides and our rapidly changing climate.

A bug hotel will attract a diverse variety of bugs and insects to your garden. They, in turn, will pollinate your plants, helping to keep your soil healthy and your plants thriving. They will also help rewild your natural space (*see* page 50).

FIND YOUR FRAME

Bug hotels must be made from untreated wood, as the treatments used on timbers are designed to repel insects. To provide structure to your hotel, repurpose something with a box-like structure and a backing, such as an old picture frame, wine crate, log or small drawer. The box shape and backing are important, as they'll help secure the items you're going to place in it (and help the bugs feel nice and cosy).

PREPARE YOUR FRAME FOR HANGING

Drill two holes in the top of the box — one slightly in from each corner. Then, take your rope, thread it through one of the holes and tie a knot at the end, making sure the knot is big enough to stop the rope from slipping through the hole. Take the other end of the string then repeat this step on the opposite hole, using scissors to trim the rope to your desired hanging length if needed. You should be left with a decent length of rope that pulls into a taut triangular shape when you hold it on a finger. It will eventually hang on a nail.

DECORATE YOUR INTERIOR

Just like us, bugs want a comfy spot to take shelter from wind and weather and lay their head after a long day of pollinating and caring for the world's plants. Fill your box with hollow bamboo poles that the insects can crawl inside. You can also use old leaves, pinecones and bark, or even cardboard rolls, which act as great hideaways for larger insects. You can also include small logs that have holes drilled into them in varying sizes to offer a secure spot for different insects. Pack the items in — there will naturally be gaps, but you don't want them rattling around.

PICK THE PERFECT SPOT

Ideally, you'll want to place your bug hotel in or near a tree — a perfectly natural environment for bugs to thrive in. You can nail your hotel to a tree trunk, but make sure it's more than 1.5m (5ft) from the ground to discourage ants, which love to feed on insect larvae. If you don't have a suitable tree, you can nail your hotel to a fence or garden shed, or mount it onto a wooden stake in your garden. Choose a spot where your hotel will get some sun but isn't too exposed to the weather. When you hang it, make sure it's stable and tilt it at a downward angle so that when it rains, the holes and crevices you've lovingly created can drain and dry out.

GROW PERENNIAL HERBS AND VEGETABLES

Growing and eating our own food is immensely satisfying.
It connects us to nature, our bodies and the seasons, but it can
be labour intensive and hard to keep up with if your life is full.
One way to make it easier is by planting perennials — plants
that grow and bear produce year after year.

Just like annual and bi-annual herbs and vegetables, perennials are nutritious and tasty. Growing them avoids the flavourlessness and food miles of much of the produce stocked in modern supermarkets, and the practice of growing them is a wonderful contributor to a lifestyle of voluntary simplicity (*see* page 10). You'll plant them just once but enjoy their harvests for years to come.

Growing perennials isn't complicated — in fact, they're great candidates for rewilding your garden (*see* page 50) as they are hardy, reliable and self-sufficient.

Perennial plants can be grown in gardens, pots and courtyards, or in a community garden if you've got one nearby. As they grow year after year, they develop strong, deep root systems that help strengthen the foundations of your soil. They're also quite robust and pest-resistant. Some, like their annual and bi-annual cousins, have specific harvesting windows, while others can be harvested all year round. Here are some perennial herbs and vegetables to consider getting started with.

JERUSALEM ARTICHOKE
Helianthus tuberosus

Jerusalem artichoke — also called sunroot, sunchoke, wild sunflower, topinambur and earth apple — is a species of sunflower that is native to central North America, but it will grow in any temperate zone. It is cultivated for its tubers, which are used as a root vegetable and can be boiled, baked and even grated fresh into salads. The tubers can be harvested four to six weeks after flowering. Even though the flowers are pretty, yields will be better if the flower buds are pinched off as they appear. Start harvesting after the first frost, when the plants begin to die back. If you're somewhere warmer, then leave harvest until mid-winter.

ASPARAGUS
Asparagus officinalis

A well-cultivated and cared for asparagus plant can provide you with edible stems for decades. However, asparagus can be picky, so ensure you plant them in a sunny spot with soil that drains well. They have a short but rewarding harvest window for six to eight weeks in spring and summer. Harvest them before the flower buds open by simply cutting or snapping off the spears at ground level.

CHIVES
Allium schoenoprasum

Chives are a great addition to many dishes, such as omelettes, potatoes, salads, soups, dips and seafood. It is a hardy, vigorous plant, so don't worry about cutting off too much. Chives also flower, attracting bees and other pollinators (*see* page 64) to your garden. When well cared for, chive plants can live for decades and can be harvested all year round.

RHUBARB
Rheum rhabarbarum

It is said that a single rhubarb plant can last 20 years. Once you've left your rhubarb plant to establish roots for one year (this is essential for their lifespan), you can harvest their stems for delicious jams and sauces. Ensure you avoid consuming the leaves, as they are poisonous. It can be harvested in spring, summer and autumn but is best left to rest in winter.

SORREL
Rumex acetosa

One of the lesser-known leafy green vegetables, sorrel is a zingy and lemony addition to salads that is also full of nutrients, such as: vitamins A, B and C, magnesium, iron, potassium and manganese. The leaves are best eaten when young and tender. Sorrel produces all year and flowers in the late spring.

CLOVE BASIL
Ocimum gratissimum

This basil lasts longer than other basils. It has smaller leaves than sweet basil, tall purple flowers and a clove-like smell. It will do best in the warmest part of your garden and may die if exposed to too much cold or frost. They do well in pots, as you can move them closer to the house or inside in winter. Its leaves can be harvested all year round.

71

NEIGHBOURHOOD
LIFE

REDUCE YOUR CARBON FOOTPRINT

Your carbon footprint is the total amount of harmful greenhouse gases, including carbon dioxide and methane, that are generated by the way you live on the Earth. Here are some practical ways to reduce your impact on the environment in the place where change starts: your local neighbourhood.

You're most likely familiar with the various calls to action of the growing environmental activism movement — from 'think global, act local' and 'act globally, act locally' to 'carbon offsetting' and 'treading lightly'. Likewise, there are different terms that allude to the crisis itself, such as 'climate change', 'global warming' and 'the global climate crisis'.

They all point to the same thing: there has never been a time in history when it is more crucial that we all do what we can to cut greenhouse gas emissions and keep global temperatures from rising more than 1.5°C. This is the target set and agreed to by more than 196 parties in the Paris Agreement of 2016.

We are all simultaneously global citizens and participants in our local communities, and we each have a role to play in tackling the climate and environmental crises that have been accelerating since the modernisation of our world. Taking these steps will help reduce your carbon footprint.

REDUCE, REUSE, RECYCLE

By living with only what we truly need (*see* page 10) and reusing and recycling wherever possible, we can significantly reduce the toll of human consumption on the Earth. For example, the fashion industry, especially 'fast fashion' — inexpensive clothing produced rapidly by mass-market retailers in response to the latest trends, often in an environmentally and ethically unsound way — is the planet's third largest polluter (after food and construction). 'Reduce, reuse, recycle' is a useful philosophy to guide your approach to goods and consumption.

- Use reusable containers, coffee cups, straws and bags to avoid unnecessary plastic from ending up in a landfill and the natural environment.

- Wear and love the clothes you have or buy second-hand instead of buying fast fashion. Buy quality and learn to mend.

- Help reduce food waste by starting to grow your own food (*see* page 68), eating seasonally (*see* page 26), shopping at local farmers' markets and composting your food scraps (*see* page 53).

- Get to know the recycling program organised by your local government or recycling provider and take part.

- Shop at stores and support brands that offer an in-store recycling program — they're growing!

- Keep packaging, glass jars and plastic bags and use them around the house. Glass jars, for example, make great recycled fridge and freezer storage containers — you just need to leave a gap between the top of the food and the top of the jar for freezer storage, as the content will expand with freezing.

PLANTS FIRST

Animal agriculture is a large contributor to greenhouse gas emissions worldwide. It's also a leading contributor to deforestation and water and air pollution, and is the leading driver of biodiversity loss. It's time to shift to a local, seasonal plant-based diet (see page 26 for more information on seasonal eating).

- Shift away from red meat, such as beef and lamb, and towards white meats, such as cruelty-free chicken and sustainably caught fish. When you do buy meat, go for organic, grass-fed meat and sustainably caught or farmed seafood.

- Introduce plant-based, nutrient- and protein-rich foods to your diet, like tofu, beans, chickpeas, oats, leafy greens, nuts and seeds.

- Eat seasonally. Head to your local greengrocer or farmers' market to see what's in season, and enjoy fruits and vegetables that have been grown close to home.

GETTING FROM A TO B

It's no secret that cars are a huge contributor to carbon emissions in the modern world. In the US, car travel accounts for a third of all air pollution, while air travel is responsible for 12 per cent transportation emissions. Happily, electric vehicles are on the rise — but there are other simple, low-carbon options we can turn to as well.

- Opt to walk instead of taking a short drive. It will do wonders for your body (see page 8), mind, wallet and the planet.

- Pull out your old bicycle and ride to your destination. Feel the exhilaration and enjoy your journey knowing you're emitting zero carbon!

- Choose public transportation over driving. It takes cars off the road and buys you time to read or daydream.

- Aim to take flights only for special occasions. We can now digitally connect multiple people from all around the world in virtual meetings, so save the carbon emissions and the airfare, and opt for a digital hangout instead.

BE COMMUNITY-CENTRIC

When working together, communities around the world can achieve incredible change, and indeed already have.

- Find a local environment group that takes part in tree planting, litter pick-ups and conservation.

- If you must commute to work, consider joining a carpooling group or taking public transportation to help reduce the vehicle load on the road (and atmosphere).

- Establish a community garden or compost bin (see page 53) with your neighbours. Growing and sharing food with others is a fantastic way to get to know your community and prioritise community health, wellbeing and the natural environment.

- Organise a share economy that brings your community together — if you need a particular tool for some DIY, borrow it from your neighbour. When we pool resources, we reduce consumption — and who knows, you might just make some new friends along the way.

- Support small local business when possible.

- Pick up trash on your local walk.

MAKE SEED BOMBS

Making seed bombs is a fun and productive way to get your hands dirty and add a little (or a lot) of beauty to your world. Throw, conceal, dig or just gently set them in places that could use a little love — think vacant lots and random patches of public dirt.

GATHER

CLAY

NATIVE SEEDS

COMPOST

POTTING MIX OR WORM CASTINGS

WATER

Seed bombs were created by members of the guerrilla gardening movement: green-thumbed city dwellers around the world who have taken it upon themselves to rewild and beautify neglected plots of land since the 1970s.

It's a positive, productive and community-focused thing to do. When we rewild and green up our urban spaces, we mitigate the effects of pollution and reduce a phenomenon known as the urban heat island effect, which refers to heat trapped in built-up areas. It also helps promote mental and physical health in urban residents by aiding psychological relaxation and stress alleviation, stimulating social cohesion, supporting physical activity, and reducing exposure to air pollutants, noise and excessive heat.

Seed bombs are simple constructions of clay (*see* page 152 for tips on how to find and dig for clay), water, compost (*see* page 53) or potting mix (or even worm castings) and native seeds. They're relatively cheap to create and make for a fun afternoon project.

The seeds of native wildflowers (*see* page 54) and plants are the most desirable for seed bombing, as they will grow well without a lot of tending. They also won't crowd out other plants, disrupt bird and insect populations or do other environmental damage. Autumn is the best time to prepare and plant seed bombs, as they will germinate over winter and flower the following spring.

METHOD

1. Lay your clay, seeds (a mixture of seeds or just one type) and compost out on a surface that you don't mind getting a little dirty.

2. Divide them into five parts clay, one part compost (or potting mix or worm castings) and one part seeds.

3. Next, combine the clay and the compost. The clay might be tough until you've warmed it with your hands, so don't be afraid to get stuck in. Adding a drop or two of water can help make it more pliable but be careful not to overdo it; the mixture should be malleable but not too sloppy. Carefully add more water if you need to, one drop at a time, and rub it all together until it becomes a gritty, dough-like mixture.

4. Add the seeds and gradually work them in, using the same rubbing and kneading method.

5. Divide the mixture and roll it into balls about the size of a nectarine.

6. You can plant your seed bombs while they are moist or let them dry. As long as they are watered once they're planted — either by you or by the rain — the clay will break down and the seeds will germinate.

KEEP A
NATURE
JOURNAL

Nature journaling is the process of writing down your observations in and about nature — think plants, birds, trees, the changing seasons and the weather — on paper. It's a simple and effective way to hone your ability to slow down, tune in to the world around you and notice ecological patterns.

Starting a nature journal is a rewarding way to build, maintain and deepen your connection with nature, and you can use it to observe, ponder and record the beauty, life and transformation taking place in the natural world around you. It also acts as a useful reference point in your rewilding journey.

There are two main types of journaling: field journaling and memory journaling. Field journaling is what you do outside and in the moment when you're immersed in a natural environment. Memory journaling is nature journaling you do after you come back from an experience outside.

Some of the world's greatest naturalists, botanists and scientists kept nature journals, including the famed English naturalist, biologist and geologist Charles Darwin and Robert Fortune, a Scottish botanist who journeyed into China to learn more about tea production for the East India Company. Both maintained extensive journaling practices in which they made observations, noted patterns and developed theories.

You might write about what you see in your garden or neighbourhood as the seasons change, make notes about growing perennials (*see* page 68) that will be helpful reference points as the years go on or simply enjoy sketching a vista that's pleasing when you stop to rest on a hike and take in your surroundings.

PONDER YOUR JOURNALING

What does nature journaling mean to you? Do you want to chronicle wild plants and animals that you encounter in the field? Do you want to reflect on how you felt while in nature? Do you want to make notes about the practise of rewilding your garden (see page 50) or growing a wildflower meadow (see page 54) or the insects that visit your bug hotel (see page 64)? Nature journaling is whatever you want it to be.

CHOOSE YOUR JOURNAL

Find a dedicated notebook to use for your nature journaling. Select one that appeals to you visually and feels good to hold. It might have lined pages or blank pages, or a mixture of both — choose lined for writing and blank pages for sketching. If you want to do a bit of both, then you'll want ... a bit of both. A hardcover journal will give you a built-in surface to write and draw on when out and about, and will stand up to the rigours of being transported in a backpack and taken out in nature.

TAKE INVENTORY

Every day in nature is different. On the days that you spend outdoors, try to paint a picture of that moment in time. What time of day is it? What is the weather like? How is the light? What can you see and smell (see page 4 for more information on tuning into your senses)? Is it noisy or quiet? By logging your experiences in nature on a particular day, you'll be able to transport yourself back there and create a useful point of comparison for the future. Imagine returning to the same spot exactly a week, month or year later, for example. Won't it be fascinating to compare your entries?

BE FREE

In addition to being a useful tool for backyard naturalism, a journal can also be a personal and private space where you can experiment and be vulnerable. Enjoy the process of capturing your experiences and memories of nature. Try your hand at drawing a flower you spot or write a story about the life of an animal whose trail you passed (see page 128 for more information on how to spot wildlife). Note your deepest thoughts and feelings alongside your observations of nature. Enjoy the process and don't worry about the final product.

STAY CURIOUS

Nature is a big mystery, and there are so many questions we want answered. Once you've arrived back home, your field journaling can become a tool for further learning and reflection. Perhaps you want to identify a plant you saw or you're wondering about the migratory patterns of a bird that has arrived in the local ecosystem and want to look it up. You might reflect on your adventure with some memory journaling. Stay curious and continue the practice of learning, observing and journaling about nature. It can become a lifelong pleasure.

PLANT A TREE

Trees play a vital role in local ecosystems and the environment as a whole. They create habitats, support biodiversity, improve air quality and provide cooling shade and green spaces. Fruit trees gift us beautiful, sweet and juicy fruits to enjoy. To start reaping the benefits, plant a tree in your garden or neighbourhood.

GATHER

POTTED TREE FOR PLANTING

WHEELBARROW OR BUCKET

SHOVEL

COMPOST

ORGANIC MULCH

GARDEN FORK

Even if you have little space or soil to plant a tree, it's possible. You can often find dwarf varieties, especially for fruit trees, at nurseries, so do a bit of research and plant a tree that will work in your space.

SELECT A TREE

What kind of tree would you like to nurture? Selecting a tree type that will eventually flower and bear fruit or other edibles (like olives or nuts) is one way to go. You might also research native trees and select one that will help rewild your garden (*see* page 50). Whichever type you choose, planting a tree will benefit your health and help tackle the climate crisis (*see* page 76).

FIND A SPOT

Ensure you find a bed for your tree where there is healthy soil, good sunlight and shelter from strong wind. Feel the soil for moisture and check if it's loamy — not too sandy, not too much clay — or simply look around to see if other plants are thriving in the area.

DIG A HOLE

Loosen the soil with the garden fork so you can easily shovel the dirt into a wheelbarrow or bucket. Create a hole that's twice as wide as your tree's pot and about 10cm (4in) deeper.

PLANT YOUR TREE

Remove your tree from its pot and gently loosen the lower roots, untangling any curled-up ones and cutting off any dead or damaged ones. This helps the tree direct all of its energy into growing new healthy roots. Place your tree into the hole you made.

NOURISH THE SOIL

Mix some compost (*see* page 53) into the soil that you dug out from the hole. This will nourish the soil and provide it with a strong foundation from which your new tree can grow. It will also help with nutrient retention when it rains. Shovel the soil back into the hole until your tree base is covered and level with the surrounding bed, ensuring it is well supported by soil on all sides, and give the soil a gentle but firm press to make sure the tree is stable. Water the tree well to let the roots and soil settle in.

CARE FOR YOUR TREE

Cover the base of your tree with some organic mulch. Wood chips, pea straw, lucerne hay or even gathered brown matter (*see* page 53) will do the trick. Make sure it's at least 10–15cm (4–6in) from the trunk and no more than 5–10cm (2–4in) deep. This will help protect the tree from weeds, retain moisture and nurture the soil. Check on your tree every week and continue to water it regularly as it grows.

PRINT LEAVES

Leaves can vary widely in size, shape and colour across plant species, and even across the same plant. They're a bit like fingerprints, in that no two leaves are exactly alike. Look closely and gather leaves that appeal to you visually, then use them as the centrepiece of your creativity.

GATHER

FRESH LEAVES

OLD NEWSPAPER

INK OR PAINT

PAPER, CARDBOARD OR FABRIC

PAINTBRUSHES OR INK SPONGES

INK BRAYER (OPTIONAL)

CLEAN CLOTH (OPTIONAL)

SMALL JAR OF WATER (OPTIONAL)

Leaf prints can be used for many decorative purposes, from creating art on archival paper or cards to customising fabric for crafting into bags, tea towels and t-shirts.

FIND THE RIGHT LEAVES

Leaves come in all shapes, sizes and textures, so look for variety as you ramble and forage. Leaves can be plucked from plants and trees to use in this project at any time of year (don't take too many!). If the tree is an evergreen, you'll need to pick them directly from the tree, even in autumn. If you are foraging for fallen autumn leaves, look for newly fallen leaves. Fresh, pliable leaves are best for this project, as dried leaves will snap and crumble when pressed or worked on.

PREPARE FOR PRINTING

Start by laying newspapers down to protect your work surface. Then lay out your paints or inks, paintbrushes or ink sponges, ink brayer (if using) and the paper or cardboard you plan to print on to. A clean cloth and a jar of water for wiping up any spills might also come in handy.

Next, prepare your masters — that's printmaking speak for the object that will create the impression you're printing: your leaves. They need to be clean and dry for your printmaking session.

PRINT THE LEAVES

Select a leaf and take a paintbrush or ink sponge and apply an even layer of paint (not too much, but enough to cover the leaf) on the side of the leaf you'd like to make an impression of. Once the leaf is fully and evenly covered, gently turn it over and press it onto the surface you want to print on. You can press it down with your hands or roll an ink brayer (roller) over its surface. When you're done, lift the leaf away slowly and admire your work.

BE PLAYFUL

You don't need to be too prescriptive with your prints, as each leaf is able to make about six. Wipe the leaf clean with a cloth between applications for the best result.

Some things to try:

· Apply a lot of paint, then a little

· Print each side of the leaf

· Push down hard when you roll or press the leaf, then push down very gently

· Hold the leaf flat to prevent movement

· Roll or press in all directions, then in just one direction

· Overlay leaf prints on top of each other.

FORAGE FOR EDIBLE WEEDS

There are hundreds of edible plants growing all around us, many of which are considered weeds. But one person's 'weed' is another's edible produce — it's all about knowing what to look for and where to look.

Thankfully, we haven't lost all our knowledge about the benefits of the plants that grow abundantly in our wild and urban environments that are often known by the unflattering name of 'weeds'. They are full of vitamins, and foraging for them can be a wonderful way to slow down, live simply (*see* page 10) and eat locally and seasonally (*see* page 22). Weeds are simply survivors — they're good at growing and will do it wherever they can. So, let's embrace their abundance and forage for and use weeds in our everyday lives.

If you suspect you have been poisoned, don't wait for symptoms to appear, seek medical attention immediately. For information call:

- Poisons Information Centre (AUS): 13 11 26

- Poison Control (USA): 1800 222 1222

- National Health Service (UK): for non-emergencies contact 111; for emergencies contact 999

FORAGE SAFELY

It's important to be sure you're foraging for weeds that are safe to eat. This is firstly about correct identification — use a handbook or a trusted app to be confident you're picking what you think you're picking. Secondly, take care to forage in areas free of pesticides or other sprays designed to destroy weeds, as ingesting these can make you ill. Roadside foraging is also best avoided, as plants can be contaminated by fumes from passing cars. You can learn more about what is safe in your area by going on a forager-led tour of local edible weeds.

Here are some nutritious edible weeds that can be found all over the world.

NETTLE
Urtica dioica

Nettle is a delicious and highly nutritious edible weed with high levels of iron and chlorophyll, and it can be enjoyed in tea or as a soup – and it can also be used to make string or cordage (*see* page 164). It is a good idea to wear gloves and even long sleeves when foraging for nettle, as it can sting you and give you an irritating rash if you brush up against it. To prepare for eating or drinking, disarm the sting of the leaves by dunking the plants into almost boiling water for 30 seconds — now you can handle nettle with ease.

MALLOW
Malva neglecta

Used as food and medicine in ancient Greece and Rome, mallow is a rich source of calcium, iron and vitamin C. Mallow can be added to savoury dishes as you would any other green leaf and is easily identifiable by the hexagonal shape of its leaves.

DANDELION
Taraxacum

One of the top six herbs in Chinese medicine, dandelion leaves have many health benefits. From being rich in vitamins A and C to purifying your blood and cleansing your liver, this weed does more than just spring up in local parks. Dandelion leaves are tasty, bitter and go nicely in salads.

BLACKBERRIES
Rubus fruticosus L. agg

For the sweetest (and arguably most delicious!) edible weed, look no further than blackberry bushes. Identified as a superfood, thanks to its richness in vitamins B and C, blackberries can be enjoyed on their own or turned into jams and other delicious desserts. Like nettle, it is a good idea to where gloves and even long sleeves when picking, as blackberry bushes have thorns to protect their fruits from prey.

WOOD SORREL
Oxalis

Also called sour grass, wood sorrel has a lemony flavour, is rich in vitamin C and the leaves, stems, flowers (usually yellow but can also be purple, white or pink) and immature seedpods can be eaten raw or cooked. Looking similar to clover, the three heart-shaped leaves joined together makes it easy to identify.

WILD FENNEL
Foeniculum vulgare

Much like the store-bought variety, wild fennel has an aniseed-like taste. Use the dried seeds and pollen for seasoning and the fronds and stalks for salads and savoury dishes.

'WHAT IS A WEED?
   A PLANT WHOSE
VIRTUES HAVE
NOT YET BEEN
     DISCOVERED,'

WROTE AMERICAN ESSAYIST, LECTURER, PHILOSOPHER,
ABOLITIONIST AND POET RALPH WALDO EMERSON.

EXTRACT DYES FROM PLANTS

People have been extracting pigments from plants and using them to make dyes to colour natural fabrics like wool, cotton and silk for thousands of years. Try your hand at this art to appreciate the beauty and vibrancy of nature's colour palette, and tune into the botanical world around you.

GATHER

ALUM POWDER

WATER

CREAM OF TARTAR

WHITE VINEGAR

RUBBER GLOVES

DRIED OR FRESH PLANT MATTER

LARGE POT

STRAINER

LARGE BOWL OR SECOND POT

FABRIC

LARGE SPOON

TOWEL

PLANTS AND COLOURS

Dye can be extracted from dried plant materials, like roots and hardwood chips, and fresh plant materials, like leaves and flowers, and you can experiment with any plant to see what colour you can draw from it. Here are some colours and the plants that are commonly used to create them:

- Blue – red cabbage, blueberries, blackberries
- Green – nettle, spinach
- Orange – yellow onion, dandelion heads
- Purple – elderberries, red or black mulberries
- Pink – strawberries, cherries, red or pink roses
- Red – hibiscus or sumac flowers
- Yellow – dandelion heads, marigold, daffodils and goldenrod flowers

EXTRACT AND PREPARE THE DYE

Fresh plant matter – cut your material into small pieces and put them in a pot, then cover them with warm water. Bring the mixture to a boil then reduce it to simmer for at least half an hour. Bear in mind that the colour will be lighter once it has dried on the fabric, so it needs to look darker than your desired end colour. Strain the liquid through a strainer into a heat resistant pot or bowl. This is the dye.

Dry plant matter – soak the dry plant matter overnight and follow the steps outlined for fresh materials above, adding extra water.

Note that you can use your dye mixture for several dyeing sessions. It can be drained, cooled and re-used immediately, or stored in the fridge until it goes mouldy.

SELECTING FABRIC AND PREPARING FOR DYEING

Wool, cotton and silk are all able to take natural dyes. To get the best results, treat them with a mordant before or after dyeing. This helps to 'fix' the colour in the fabric and stops it from rinsing out when you wash the fabric. The ancients used alum (aluminium powder) as a mordant, and so can you. You can buy it at most chemists (drugstores). Together with cream of tartar and water (the recommended amounts vary by fabric type), you effectively dye the fabric in the mordant and let it dry dyeing dying in the actual dye bath.

DYEING AND DRYING YOUR FABRIC

Wet your fabric by quickly submerging it in clean water (no need to wring it), then place it in the simmering dye bath. Let it continue to simmer on the stove for about 30 minutes – or until it is the desired colour (the longer you leave it in the dye bath, the deeper the colour will get). Gently stir it from time to time to ensure the colour is distributed evenly. When you are satisfied, drain the dye (use container if you want to save it) and rinse the fabric well in cool water, then lay it flat on an old towel to dry.

SAFETY NOTES

Always wear rubber gloves when handling dyes, dyed fabrics and mordants, and never use your gloves, dye vessels or spoons for cooking.

GO ON A MICROADVENTURE

Not all adventures have to reach far and wide — there are plenty of opportunities for discovery and new experiences close to home. Introducing the microadventure: a small and achievable adventure that is possible to fit into even the busiest of schedules.

It was contemporary adventurer and author Alastair Humphreys who coined the charming term 'microadventure'. Being an adventure that is short, simple, local and cheap, a microadventure can (and should) still be fun, exciting, challenging, refreshing and rewarding.

Adventures are fantastic for our soul. They challenge our minds and bodies in new ways and bring a sense of wonder and discovery into our lives. When shared with others, adventures are a source of joy and quality time, allowing you to work together for a shared experience or outcome.

One of the great appeals of microadventures is that they make adventuring accessible to anyone, anywhere — there's no need to have a lot of outdoor experience or gear.

A dog can be a wonderful microadventure companion, as can the beauty of solitude. Get creative with your microadventures and make them suit your interests. Look for street art on your walk, go on a photo safari or take a turn you've never taken before. Keep an eye out for plants to propagate (see page 46); collect wildflowers or leaves for ikebana arrangements, leaf prints or natural dyes (see pages 60, 90, 98), or forage for edible weeds (see page 92). Here are some more ideas to consider.

HOST A BACKYARD SLUMBER PARTY

Feel like breaking out of your four walls but don't want to venture into the wilderness? Pitch a tent in the backyard and host a slumber party. If it's permitted, build a fire (see page 132) to sit around together. Tell flashlight stories and identify the sounds of your neighbourhood at night. Feel a sense of adventure with your house as the backdrop.

TAKE A WILD SWIM

Taking a swim in a natural body of water ignites our senses and invigorates our bodies (for more information, see pages 144, 176). Is there a river, lake or beach near you where it is safe to swim? Take yourself outside your comfort zone and enjoy a plunge. You'll emerge feeling refreshed, invigorated, connected with nature and with your own sense of adventure.

ENJOY A MOONLIGHT STROLL

How often do you enjoy your neighbourhood by moonlight? We often forget about the nightly world coming to life outside: the nocturne. Take yourself and a companion out on a moonlight walk, and notice how the world changes at night. Look out for the glow of stars (see page 200), perhaps spot some nocturnal creatures like owls or bats (see page 128 for more information on how to spot wildlife) and see your neighbourhood with new, darkness-adapted eyes.

IMMERSE YOURSELF IN THE SEASONS AND CYCLES OF NATURE

You can also create microadventures around the seasons and cycles of nature. Go cloudspotting (see page 102), splash in puddles or get out and smell the rain. Plan to be outdoors to see a blue moon (see page 28 to learn how to identify the different moon phases) or the annual Perseid meteor shower to witness nature on full display. Ultimately, you want to remind yourself that simply being in nature can be a great adventure.

PREDICT
THE
WEATHER

Look up and watch the clouds. What do you see? Learning to identify the clouds can help you predict, understand and prepare for the weather, and also deepen your understanding of the world around you.

In the past, people knew the clouds well and understood what their appearance and behaviour meant for the weather, farm management and food. The form, shape and density of the clouds, how high they sit in the sky, their colour and where and how fast they're moving are all portents of atmospheric and environmental things to come.

Today we rely on meteorologists and weather forecasters to tell us what the weather is going to be like. These scientists develop local and regional weather forecasts for several days into the future, using technology such as weather satellites and Doppler radar to track and predict weather events happening over a broad region. With a bit of learning and observation, it's possible to make relatively accurate predictions for yourself.

THE WEATHER SYSTEM AND HOW IT WORKS

'Weather' is the mix of events – from warm sun and a cooling breeze to grey clouds, rain and snow – that happen in the atmosphere. Most weather happens in the part of Earth's atmosphere that is closest to the ground, which is called the troposphere. The average weather pattern that occurs over a number of years or decades is what we call 'climate'.

Daily weather events are controlled by changes in air pressure, which is in turn caused by the weight of the air molecules that make up the atmosphere.

When air pressure is high, the skies are blue and clear, as high pressure causes air to flow downwards and fan out when it gets near the ground, preventing clouds from forming. Conversely, when the air pressure is low, air flows together and then upward where it gathers, rises, cools and forms clouds.

TYPES OF CLOUDS

Look up, what do you see? Common clouds come in ten different types. They each have different shapes, occur at different altitudes and can be grouped and understood based on either variable (shape or altitude).

The cloud names are Latin and comprise either adjectives that describe their shape or combinations of adjectives and prefixes that describe their nature or place in the sky.

Cumulo – meaning 'heaped' – are puffy, marshmallow-like clouds

Strato – meaning 'layered' – are clouds that are often flat and form a wide layer across the sky

Nimbo – meaning 'rain' – are dark, murky clouds that produce rain

Cirro – meaning 'curl' – are clouds that are often curly but can also appear wispy and streaky

Alto – meaning 'high' – are clouds that occur at a mid-level altitude.

LOW CLOUDS – CUMULONIMBUS, CUMULUS, STRATUS AND STRATOCUMULUS

Sitting below 2000m (6560ft) in the sky are the low-level clouds that seem close and sometimes heavy. Low-level clouds can form either horizontally or vertically. The horizontal varieties are likely to be grey or murky sheets across the sky and often bring rain. The vertical variety are much more cartoon-like and appear as fluffy blobs in the sky.

Cumulonimbus is a tall, fluffy cloud that can turn dark and stormy quite quickly. Cumulus is the fluffy cotton-ball variety that often peppers the blue sky. Stratus is a low, grey sheet cloud that can turn into fog. Stratocumulus are thicker, dark grey clumps of cloud, but they don't bring rain.

Weather indicator: rain approaching/ dark and stormy weather ahead / fog likely

MID-LEVEL CLOUDS – ALTOCUMULUS, ALTOSTRATUS AND NIMBOSTRATUS

Sitting between 2000–6000m (6000–20,000ft), mid-level clouds can contain water droplets, ice crystals or both. Often quite thick and sheet-like, these clouds can block out the sun and signal that rain or snow is approaching.

Altocumulus clouds are fluffy clouds that clump into groups resembling cotton balls. Altostratus is a classic, grey, featureless sheet of cloud that can mask the sky and sun and indicate that a storm is on its way. Nimbostratus is a dark and featureless cloud that covers the sky – when you see this cloud, it's likely already raining.

Weather indicator: rain or snow approaching / storm ahead / it's raining

HIGH CLOUDS – CIRRUS, CIRROCUMULUS AND CIRROSTRATUS

Often spotted at the top of mountains or from outside the window of your aeroplane, cirrus clouds sit higher in the sky than any other variety. Sitting at above 6000m (20,000ft), the cold atmospheric temperature leads to the cirrus clouds being composed of mostly ice crystals, meaning they're not carrying rain.

The various cirrus clouds are light, feathery and often create a thin blanket-like cover over the sky, sometimes appearing like a painting with long brushstrokes. Their thinness still allows sunlight to pass through, which sometimes creates a halo-like light reflection off the clouds' ice crystals.

Weather indicator: fair weather

FOREST LIFE

GO ON
A HIKE

Hikes are long walks in natural settings, like forests, and often come with elevation changes and dynamic terrains. A step up (and out) from casual walking in urban environments or along paved trails, hiking is an invigorating way to immerse yourself in nature.

Hiking can be done over the course of a day, overnight or over several nights and on long, arduous pilgrimages. Going on a hike is a breathtaking way to get out of the city and immerse yourself in nature, be it solo, with friends or as part of an organised group or tour.

Forests are rich with nature, life and adventure. They're complex ecosystems full of old-growth trees that showcase Earth's history. There are many ways to hike and explore awe-inspiring natural environments. Whether you're starting out on your first hike or you're an experienced overnighter, make sure to hike at a level of difficulty that suits you.

It's likely that suitable locations for day and overnight hikes are closer to home than you might think. On a map, look for local state or national parks and forests and mountain areas where you can spend a day or two exploring. Research nearby trails to ensure they're your desired length and suit your fitness level. Most cities and towns provide guides on where you can hike in the local area and where the best spots for overnight camping are.

When camping overnight or leaving your campsite unattended, such as when you're going for a hike or swim, securing your food where animals can't reach it will give you peace of mind (and breakfast). Bag your food, toothpaste, lotions and anything else that smells inviting and string it up in a tree — this will make it harder for animals to explore your stash while you sleep.

DAY HIKES

Day hikes are a great place to start because you don't need to carry shelter or food for several days, but they still give you enough time to explore and experience a day in nature. Take yourself on a few day hikes to familiarise yourself with prolonged walking and being outdoors.

PACKING AND SAFETY LIST

- Enough water for the day — you'll need more than you think! Check if there is drinking water available on the trail. Consider bringing water filters or cleaning tablets if natural water sources are available along the way.

- A map of the area and a compass (*see page 114*). Remember, there isn't always mobile reception in nature.

- Nutritious, energy-boosting snacks, such as trail mix and protein balls, to help build up and slowly release energy reserves in your body.

- A good pair of worn-in hiking boots or comfortable walking shoes.

- Check the weather and dress appropriately — if it's sunny, you'll need sunglasses; a hat; a thin, lightweight shirt and sunscreen. If it's due to rain, a waterproof jacket or poncho and gaiters (waterproof boot covers) will help keep you comfortable.

- A small first-aid kit and any personal medications you might need.

- Always tell someone where you are going and when you plan to be back.

OVERNIGHT HIKES

If you're confident as a day hiker and are ready for an adventure, try an overnight hike. Overnight hikes let you travel further and deeper into nature, and you'll experience camping under the stars (*see* page 118). Remember to plan hikes that are achievable and won't push you too far beyond your comfort zone. Test out any gear at home to make sure you can use it before you depart, and consider carrying your gear on shorter walks near home to test and build your strength for this new challenge.

PACKING AND SAFETY LIST

On top of everything you'd pack for a day hike, overnight hikes require more gear and planning to ensure you're safe and comfortable. It requires a lot more energy to walk when you're carrying all your camping gear and food, so pack as lightly as you possible can and keep this in mind when planning your route. Camping stores sell a variety of lightweight equipment for hiking, but expect to pay to shed those extra kilos in your pack.

- Tent, sleeping mat, sleeping bag, sleeping bag liner, blow-up pillow.

- Clothing for all weather.

- Enough food and water to last the whole trip. Avoid heavy foods (like cans) and consider lightweight options, like freeze-dried meals or pasta. Remember you'll need food for breakfast, lunch, dinner and snacks throughout the day.

- Cooking equipment and utensils. If you want to cook your food, you'll need a small, lightweight hiking stove and a pot to cook it in. You'll also need a bowl or plate, a mug and a fork and/or spoon (or a spork!) for each person.

- Matches or steel and flint set (*see* page 132) and a flashlight or headlamp.

PILGRIMAGES

Pilgrimages are hikes designed for the most seasoned walkers. Often spanning hundreds and sometimes even thousands of kilometres, pilgrimages have been walked for generations and often have religious origins. A modern-day pilgrim need not have a faith-based religion to experience one of these lengthy trails; a desire to challenge and immerse oneself in nature is motivation enough.

PACKING LIST

- Pilgrimages are well-established routes that are often set up with guesthouses along the way. Plan ahead and decide whether you want to pack (and carry) a tent and all the things you need to set up camp or arrange to sleep in the comfort of a real bed at night.

- When walking long distances, fatigue is natural. Think about what you can pack (and leave behind!) to make your hike easier. Perhaps trekking poles will help you feel lighter and hit your stride, but your big camera will weigh you down. Pack light and only bring the essentials.

- As on all hikes, you need to be prepared for all types of weather. Pack for wet, dry, warm and cool weather, prioritising moisture-wicking, lightweight materials that are multi-purpose and can be layered in cooler environments.

112

THREE ICONIC TRAILS

Appalachian Trail, United States
Dubbed the world's longest hiking-only trail, the Appalachian runs north to south along the East Coast of the US, passing through mainly forest and mountain regions of 14 different states.

Length: 3570 kilometres [2200 miles]
Time: 5–7 months

El Camino de Santiago, Spain
A series of routes that all arrive in Santiago in northern Spain, this was a popular pilgrimage for medieval Christians who travelled to the shrine of the apostle Saint James the Great. The most popular starting place is Saint-Jean-Pied-de-Port in the south of France.

Length: 800 kilometres [500 miles]
Time: 1 month

Pilgrim's Way, England
Following a trail that probably existed during the Stone Age, this trail was popularised by 12th-century pilgrims trekking to the resting site of the martyr and former Archbishop of Canterbury Thomas Beckett.

Length: 245 kilometres [153 miles]
Time: 15 days

113

NAVIGATE WITH A COMPASS AND MAP

No matter where you are in the world, a compass will point north and can help you find your way, even in the remotest locations. Increase your self-sufficiency by learning how to navigate using a compass and map and how to make your own simple compass.

be handled and stored carefully (away from magnets!) to retain their usefulness. Follow this guide to learn how to use a compass.

LINE UP YOUR 'FROM' AND 'TO' POINTS

Start by identifying where you are on the map (point A) and where you want to go (point B). Lay your map out flat and use the side of your compass or one of the black lines running down its base plate to line up point A and point B. Ignore the compass needle at this stage, but make sure that the direction of the compass' travel arrow is pointing in the direction you want to go (towards point B).

ALIGN TO GRID NORTH

Keeping your compass still, turn the housing bezel so that the 'N' on the bezel and the orienteering arrow are pointing to the top of the map. This is 'grid north' (not to be confused with true north). Continue to ignore the compass needle, but, to ensure accuracy, make sure the orienteering lines on the compass are lined up with the easting lines on the map.

ADJUST FOR MAGNETIC VARIATION

Next up, you need to adjust for the difference between magnetic north and grid north. This will depend on where you are in the world and is often considered the most challenging aspect of using a compass. To work out what the correct adjustment for your location is, look for 'magnetic north' in your map's key. Then turn your compass bezel anticlockwise to add any positive magnetic variations required, or clockwise if they need to be subtracted. To make this task easier, most compasses provide a smaller scale inside the compass housing, but you can also use the outer scale.

When spending time in nature, it's best not to rely too much on online maps and navigation tools; batteries can go flat and signals can be lost. All hail the handy compass.

A store-bought compass uses a magnet to align its needle to the Earth's magnetic field. The best way to visualise this is to imagine a magnetic pole stretching from the top to the bottom of the globe. One type of magnet sits to the north and another to the south. The rule with magnets is that 'opposites attract', so the magnet in your compass is the opposite charge to the one in the North Pole, leading your compass to be attracted and shift its needle to the north.

While amazing and very handy, the Earth's magnetic field is not particularly strong. This is why you often see compasses made of very light materials, with the needle floating on a well-oiled axis. This allows even the faintest magnetic attraction to activate your compass and help you find your way. It also means compasses should

IDENTIFY THE DIRECTION OF TRAVEL AND FIND A WAYPOINT

Put away your map, taking care not to move the compass bezel. It's helpful to have a friend or hiking companion who can do this for you! Hold the compass so that it is level and close to your body, with the 'direction of travel' arrow pointing straight ahead. Slowly turn around, keeping the compass as still as possible, until the red end of the needle lines up with the orienting arrow. The travel arrow should still point straight ahead – that's the way you are going: towards B.

Now pick an object in the distance that's in same direction as point B. It could be an interestingly shaped tree or rock, an old farmhouse or a hill. Start walking towards the waypoint you've selected. Once you've reached it, you can check the compass again, pick a new distinctive object to walk towards, and carry on.

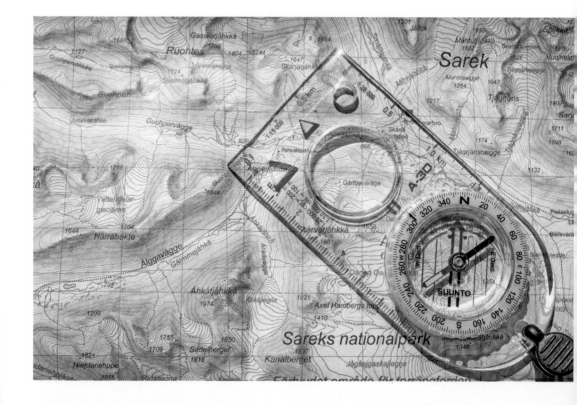

HOW TO MAKE AND USE YOUR OWN COMPASS

Compasses are relatively simple and fun to make, and knowing how to make one on the fly might just come in handy one day.

GATHER

SEWING NEEDLE

SMALL MAGNET

CRAFT KNIFE

SMALL PIECE OF CORK

PLIERS

SHALLOW BOWL

WATER

METHOD

1. First, you'll need to magnetise the needle. Do this by rubbing your magnet along the needle several times in one direction only, from needle eye to tip.

2. Use the knife to cut a thin circle of cork, about 0.6cm (1/4in) thick.

3. Push the needle as far as you can into the centre of the cork lengthwise by hand, then use the pliers to push the needle right through, taking care to ensure the needle is sticking out of both ends of the cork evenly.

4. Fill the bowl halfway with water and gently place the cork and needle on the surface.

5. Ensure your compass is set up on a flat surface and watch as your magnetised needle spins to point north.

6. Now, test out your compass and see if you can orient yourself on a map! Figure out which way is north or south and go from there.

CAMP
OUTSIDE

Going camping is a fulfilling adventure for people young and old.
Out in nature, you can look forward to slowing down and attuning
yourself to your surroundings — waking early to birdsong and
sitting around a fire spotting stars at night.

There are many different places to go camping, from off-the-trail free camps and bush camps to organised, amenity-filled camping grounds, where you sometimes have to book weeks or even months in advance. You might camp alongside a creek or river or in a forest clearing. You might even sleep fully outside, with only the starry sky as your roof. If you're seeking a microadventure (*see* page 100), you can also camp in your — or a friend's — backyard.

BORROW OR MAKE DO

If you don't already have camping gear, try to borrow equipment or make use of what you already have. Here's a basic packing list:

· Mattress or comfortable base to sleep on, like a yoga mat. Even couch cushions can do the trick.

· A sheet, pillow and sleeping bag or bedding of choice.

· Shelter (if desired) — a tent or bivouac are common choices.

· Food and cooking equipment. Bring a cooler box (or a car fridge if you've got one) to keep your food cold.

· Headlamps or flashlights (and batteries) and a lantern (and mantles and fuel/ batteries), if needed.

· Camp chairs and table (optional).

· Sunscreen and bug spray.

· First-aid kit.

· Personal medications.

· Matches or steel and flint to light your fire (*see* page 132 to learn how to build a fire). Check if the area you're going to is likely to have firewood (and if you're allowed to take it off the ground) or bring your own.

CHOOSE YOUR SPOT

Sleeping outdoors is a straightforward enough idea, but there are a few things you can do to make sure your sleep and overall experience are as comfortable as possible. Try to pitch your tent or lay your mattress on flat ground — even the gentlest of inclines can make you feel a bit skewwhiff. If you do have to camp on an incline, ensure your head is elevated above your feet so you don't wake up with a headache. Don't sleep across to the incline — you'll roll. Clear the ground of any stones or twigs, and make sure you aren't setting up underneath any overhanging branches — dead or alive. Avoid setting up close to big roads if you can, and if you're sharing the space with others, give yourselves space to spread out. Lastly, think about where you want to be in relation to the rising sun in the morning — if it's going to be cold you might want to be in its path, but if it's going to warm up quickly, you might prefer a spot with morning shade.

119

BE A FRIENDLY NEIGHBOUR

If you're camping near other people, be
sure to follow basic camping etiquette.
Keep noise to a minimum so both you and
your neighbours can enjoy the sounds of
nature without disruption. Finally, keep a
considerate distance if walking through or
around your neighbour's campsite. If your
neighbours follow the same etiquette, you
won't feel like you have neighbours at all.

LEAVE NO TRACE

There's a saying that when we're in
nature we should take only memories and
leave only footprints. When camping, be
mindful of the native wildlife and vegetation.
If you're allowed to build fires, take care
to do so responsibly (*see* page 132). Take
all your trash with you, even the organic
waste. If you're going to the bathroom in
nature, make sure you bury your waste
at least 20cm (8in) deep and more than
100m (40ft) from water sources. By
caring for the environment when we
spend time outdoors, we can preserve it
for future visits and other nature lovers.

'I HAVE STOPPED
SLEEPING INSIDE.
A HOUSE IS TOO SMALL,
TOO CONFINING.
I WANT THE WHOLE WORLD,
AND THE
STARS TOO.'

SUE HUBBELL
A COUNTRY YEAR

WHITTLE A WALKING STICK

Blades, knives and sharp implements have long been tools for carving and shaping objects out of wood. Whittling is the simple, meditative practice of shaving away slivers from a piece of wood — either simply for the time-passing joy of it or to make something useful, like a walking stick.

GATHER

KNIFE

WOOD TO SUIT YOUR PROJECT

METAL SCRAPER (OPTIONAL)

WHETSTONE OR SHARPENING STEEL (OPTIONAL)

CLOTH (OPTIONAL)

WOOD STAIN OR OIL (OPTIONAL)

Whittling wood is a task anybody can pick up. The beauty of whittling is that it's not about perfection; every piece is entirely unique to the wood it is made of — and the hands that carve it.

SELECTING YOUR KNIFE

The most suitable knife for whittling is one that you find comfortable and manoeuvrable and is, crucially, sharp. Ironically, a sharp knife is safest to use, as a blunt knife requires less fine skill and more brute force, reducing precision and increasing the chances of the knife slipping and cutting you. Ideally it will have a blunt edge on one side so you can put your thumb on it and guide the knife as you carve.

MAINTAINING YOUR BLADE

Whittling knives can dull quite quickly. A whetstone is the simplest tool for sharpening and comes with two sides: a coarse side for sharpening and a smoother side for finishing. Angling the sharp edge of the blade slightly downwards, lay it on the coarse side of the whetstone and draw it toward you. Do this several times on both sides of the blade until you feel it has been sufficiently sharpened. Repeat the same movement on the smooth side of the stone. Wipe your blade with a cloth to finish the process. If you don't have a proper whetstone, you can use a sharpening steel, or, if you're really in a pinch, try using a nail file, a leather belt, the edge of a coffee mug or even a glass bottle to sharpen your blade.

SELECT YOUR CARVING MATERIALS

Working with a natural material like wood can make whittling unpredictable, as different tree species produce different types of wood. Some are denser than others, some have more sap, some are prone to splitting and some are just right. Fresh, green wood is the softest and easiest to work with, but sometimes releases a sticky sap that can present challenges. In contrast, seasoned wood that has dried and hardened is more difficult to carve and can be prone to splitting. Aim to find a wood that lands somewhere in the middle.

UNDERSTAND THE GRAIN

Every piece of wood is different, thanks to the grain of fibres that runs through every tree from trunk to crown. Working with wood that has a straight, regular grain is much easier and more predictable than working with a curvy, coarse grain. Regardless, ensure you're always carving in the same direction as the wood's fibres. Carving against the grain will cause fibres to split, leaving an untidy finish.

125

CARVING TECHNIQUES

Stop cut — The most versatile technique and the one you'll likely use to start your project, a stop cut is a downward push on your blade to create marks in the surface of your wood. These marks will help guide your future carves.

Pull cut — Holding your knife in position with the blade facing away from you, pull your wood against the blade, making a smooth, safe cut.

Push cut — Used to round off edges and carve notches into the wood, a push cut is delivered by pushing the blade into the wood, away from your body. It can help to push the thumb of the hand holding the knife against the blade's blunt edge to move the blade along.

Paring cut — Perhaps best known as the carving technique you use to peel an apple with a knife, a paring cut will help you begin to take some of the body out of your wood. Using your thumb to steady the motion, carefully pull the blade toward your thumb, cutting a slice off the surface of the wood.

Split cut — Used on wood with a straight grain to create a split, a split cut is administered by balancing your wood upright on a flat surface and laying the blade across the top of the grain before knocking the knife downwards with a heavy piece of wood, a bit like how you use an axe (*see* page 130).

SAFETY FIRST

Remember the key knife rules:

- Never use a dull blade
- Always clean your knife after you use it
- Never carry an open pocket knife
- Keep your pocket knife dry
- Never cut towards yourself (paring cut is the exception here)

METHOD

1. Find a branch in the forest that feels right for you — one that feels nice in your hand and is the right length for your height. Try to find one that has recently fallen from the tree (look for hints of 'green' bark as a telltale sign).

2. Take your blade and, cutting away from your body, remove any smaller branches and knots.

3. Now use the stop cut to mark where you want the handle.

4. Using the pull-cut technique, begin by removing the bark to reveal the pale inner wood. Remove all the bark from the middle of the stick, before moving to either end. This will help you whittle more evenly.

5. Leave your stick to dry overnight, allowing excess moisture to evaporate. This process will also let you know where bits of inner bark have been missed, as these will oxidise and brown overnight.

6. Use your metal scraper, or the blunt edge of your knife, to remove any inner bark and create a smooth surface.

7. Using the push-cut technique, round out the edges of your stick by cutting off small pieces around the rim of the stick.

8. If you're feeling inspired, make some decorative markings; the stop cut is good for this.

9. To give your new walking stick the longest life possible, you can oil or stain it.

126

SPOT SIGNS
OF WILDLIFE

Seeing animals going about their lives in their natural habitats is one of life's great joys. Learning how to spot, identify and track signs of animal activity can help you find and observe wildlife with care and deepen your nature connection.

When spending time in nature, happening upon wild animals is an exhilarating experience. Observing animals safely and unobtrusively is fascinating and enchanting — a real gift. Hiking (*see* page 110), canoeing (*see* page 148) and camping (*see* page 118) are excellent times to keep an eye out for wildlife. Learning some telltale signs of animal activity is also great if you're a nature lover who wants to observe and appreciate animals going about their natural lives, or perhaps find some material for your nature journal (*see* page 82).

Animal tracking is practised by scientists, rangers and hunters. In hunting and ecology, it's the science and art of observing animal tracks and other signs with the goal of understanding the landscape and the animal being tracked. A further goal of tracking is the deeper understanding of the systems and patterns that make up the surrounding environment.

DO YOUR RESEARCH

It helps to have an idea of what kinds of wildlife lives in your area and do some research into what their tracks and scat (poo) look like before you head out. Consider whether you're interested in diurnal (active during the day) or nocturnal (active during the night) creatures and incorporate that into your preparation. Research online, visit the library or connect with a local animal welfare organisation.

LOOK FOR FOOTPRINTS AND SCAT

The telltale signs of an animal's presence are footprints and scat. When you spot footprints, look closely. Do the prints have the short, round toes of a cat? Or the long feet of a hare or rabbit? Could it be a hoofed creature like a deer or a goat? Or the dainty, sharp feet of a bird? Thinking about how far apart each footprint is and whether they're in groups of twos or fours can indicate size and whether they were made by a biped (two-legged) or quadruped (four-legged) creature. Follow the tracks to see where they lead.

Different species do quite distinctive poos. Australian wombats, for example, are famous for doing square-shaped poos! Learn the shapes and sizes of the various animals in your area. Scat can also give an indication of the diet (look for grass and berries) and how recently the creature was in the area.

SEEK OUT ANIMAL HIGHWAYS

Just like us, animals move through the landscape via pathways and passages they've created through the dense foliage. Fields of grass are parted, branches can be snapped and the forest floor disturbed. Once these paths have been used over and over again, they become animal highways — safe passages that animals identify and use. Look for these established tracks and see where they lead.

DECIPHER CLUES

You can find evidence of wild animals almost everywhere in the wild when you know what to look for, and these clues can help you determine if there are any animals nearby. Beyond the big-ticket clues of footprints and scat, looking for leaves, flowers and fruits that have been disturbed — or a kill — can indicate recent feeding activity in the area. Feathers on the ground or fur on bushes can indicate a tussle, a kill or simply an animal passing through. Can you spot any nests or burrows? Clues like these will help you understand what animals live or have passed through the area recently and give clues to their behaviour.

SPLIT WOOD WITH AN AXE

An axe is a tool used for chopping wood, and humans have been using them for at least 40,000 years. Typically made from iron with a sharp steel edge and a wooden handle, learning how to use one to safely split firewood is a great outdoor skill.

GATHER

A SPLITTING AXE OR MAUL

TREE STUMP TO USE AS A SPLITTING STATION

SUSTAINABLY SOURCED FIREWOOD

An axe is a big, powerful tool that must be handled with care. Focus on accuracy first, not power. Make sure you're wearing covered footwear, and always put the axe out of harm's way when you're done.

Make sure your axe is sharp, as cutting quickly, efficiently and safely with an axe requires a sharp edge. That said, it's best if it's not razor sharp, as a razor sharp edge is often more prone to chipping than a decently sharp edge. The idea is to create an edge free of nicks and dents that is sharp enough to slice through wood fibres. You can do this with a whetstone (*see* page 124) or a file.

If you want to collect your own wood, you'll need to check if it is allowed in your area and if there are any rules and regulations that apply and take care to source the wood sustainably (*see* page 133). You can also get firewood delivered by a local, sustainable supplier – this way you know your wood is coming from trees that aren't vital for the habitat and you are more likely to get high-quality firewood.

METHOD

1. Source your firewood through a local, sustainable firewood supplier, or make sure you're gathering it from a permitted area at a permitted time of year.

2. Create and clear a flat, stable splitting station. An old tree stump is perfect. Ensure that there are no obstacles above or around the station — there shouldn't be anything that could get in the way of a clear, calculated swing. As the old saying goes: 'clear the ground an axe-length around'. Ensure any onlookers stay at a safe distance, about two axe lengths away.

3. Stand with your legs about shoulder-width apart or until you feel sturdy on your feet. This keeps your legs out of the axe's way. Now pick a spot on the piece of wood where you want to chop.

4. Hold your splitting axe with your preferred hand a hand-length below the axe's head. With your other hand, hold just above the knob of the handle, with your palm facing you. Hold the axe firmly, but not too tight.

5. Lift the axe over your head and steadily swing it straight down to meet the wood at the point where you want to chop it. The momentum of your swing will propel your top hand to slide down to meet your hand at the handle — this should happen, so go with the flow. If the wood doesn't split the first time, try again, aiming to hit the exact same spot.

6. Continue till you've got a nice pile of logs. Now you're ready to build a fire (*see* page 132).

131

BUILD A FIRE

Scientists think early humans first began to control fire between 1.7–2 million years ago and consider it a defining feature of human intelligence and evolution. Learning how to safely build a fire is a fundamental outdoor skill — one that keeps you warm and enables you to cook food.

GATHER

TINDER

KINDLING

SUSTAINABLY SOURCED FUEL WOOD

MATCHES OR OTHER IGNITION SOURCE

BUCKET OF WATER

SHOVEL

Fuel, oxygen and an ignition source are the essential elements of fire, and you should plan ahead so you have them all before you begin. But first, it's vital that you ensure you're permitted to build a fire in your location and at the time of year you're in, as many reserves ban fires in summer to safeguard against wildfire. You must always have a bucket of water (at least 10 litres) next to the fire to extinguish it and be prepared in case something goes wrong and the fire starts to spread.

SOURCING WOOD SUSTAINABLY

Be responsible and protect the environment by sourcing the wood for your fire sustainably. This means never cutting wood from trees, but, if it's allowed, gathering fallen wood from the ground in the area where you're building your fire. If you're doing this, go for smaller branches that easily snap in your hands or underfoot, not logs, as fallen logs make wonderful homes for all sorts of wildlife. You can also buy and bring your own. If you're going to buy wood, try to do it somewhere close to where you are camping — this supports the local economy and helps ensure the wood ash you leave behind will not harm the local ecosystem.

CREATE YOUR FIRE PIT

Creating a designated space for your fire allows you to protect it from the elements and keep it under control. It should be in a relatively open space with no branches overhead.

Choose a location for your fire pit that is 2m (6ft) from any trees and/or your campsite. Look for a clear, dry and flat surface, choosing somewhere that is out of the wind. Clear it of leaves and other tinder.

Surround your fire bed with rocks; this will stop your fire from 'jumping' or spreading.

SOURCES OF IGNITION

Lighter or matches — Use a lighter or a match to light the tinder of the fire. Pro tip: keep these in a small waterproof box or bag so they don't accidentally get wet if you're hiking or camping.

Steel and flint — A popular, weather-proof option, steel and flint sets can be purchased from any outdoor store. Angle the steel and flint towards the tinder and strike the two together to produce a spark that lands in the tinder. Gently blow on the spark to help it ignite.

Fire plough — With a flat piece of soft wood and a pocket knife, use a stop cut then a push cut technique to carve an inch-wide groove along the grain of the wood (*see* page 124) and place some tinder at the bottom. Using a stick, begin to plough (rub) up and down the groove, towards the tinder. Eventually you will create enough friction and heat, and the wood particles in the tinder will ignite.

THE TYPES OF WOOD YOU'LL NEED

Tinder — You'll need a big handful of dry leaves, grass or bark, anything that will catch a flame easily. Tinder is often volatile and will burn quickly, so have your kindling on hand. If you can't find any dry tinder, you can use a piece of paper or a small block of fire lighter.

Kindling — This is smaller twigs and branches that will easily catch, sustain and grow your tinder's flame. These are the crucial mediators in building your fire.

Fuel wood — These are the classic branches and logs that will burn and provide sustained warmth and light to your campsite. Make sure you have fuel wood in a variety of sizes (*see* page 130 to learn how to split your own). It needs to be dry, not wet or damp, as wet or damp wood will not burn well and will create a lot of smoke. Have enough to sustain your fire for as long as you want it to burn.

METHOD

Building a fire is part art, part science. They must be built gradually, with precision and care. Always keep a bucket of water near your fire for safety and to extinguish the fire.

1. Place your tinder in the centre of your fire pit. This is where your fire will begin — but don't light it yet.

2. Criss-cross your kindling over the top of the tinder, making sure not to smother the tinder — you want to allow airflow so it doesn't suffocate and extinguish itself when you light it. You'll also need enough space for your ignition source to get to the tinder.

3. Now take your ignition source and carefully light the tinder in a few different spots. Stay close while it takes — it can help to blow gently on any small flames that catch to help them grow, but try to shield the small flames as much as possible from the wind, as it can easily blow them out.

4. Once the kindling is well alight, criss-cross two or three smaller pieces of fuel wood over the kindling.

5. Once your fire is established, you can add thicker logs that are slower to burn.

EXTINGUISH YOUR FIRE

You must ensure your fire is fully extinguished before you leave it. This applies to when you're going to bed for the night, leaving your campsite to go hiking or swimming and when heading home.

1. Begin to extinguish your fire at least 20 minutes before you leave your site to give the fire enough time to burn out while you can still supervise.

2. Break up the fire with a shovel to make it easier to put out.

3. Sprinkle some water over your fire using a watering can, bucket or bowl. Do this gently and gradually to prevent the fire from spitting.

4. To make sure every ember is doused in water, stir the fire with a larger stick or a shovel while sprinkling more water over the top. This will extinguish any hidden embers.

5. Use your hand to feel close to the base of the fire, if it feels cool the fire is likely extinguished, but also check for any sounds or steam, as these could be signs of lingering embers. If you do find these signs, repeat this process again.

FORAGE FOR MUSHROOMS

Mushrooms are neither fruits nor vegetables, but members of the fungi kingdom. There are roughly 14,000 different types — some are deadly, some are hallucinogenic and some are edible. Learning to recognise and forage for the edible ones is a delightful way to spend time in nature and add to your pantry.

GATHER

PARING KNIFE

BASKET OR CARDBOARD BOX

SOFT BRUSH FOR CLEANING

WARM CLOTHES AND GLOVES (FOR WARMTH)

Mushrooms belong in a kingdom of their own, separate from plants and animals. These fascinating organisms grow in symbiosis with each other and their environment, and their root systems are especially fascinating. Called mycelium, it's an underground mass of branching fibres or 'threads' of the greater fungal organism that wrap around or bore into tree roots. In essence, mycelium makes molecules and assembles them into large structures called mycorrhizal networks, which connects individual plants together, allowing them to communicate with each other and transfer water, nitrogen, carbon and other minerals around the network.

Since 2007, humans have been harnessing the incredible strength and growing power of mycelium as a means of more sustainable and rapid production. We use it to produce everything from plastic alternatives and plant-based meat to scaffolding for growing organs. Like mushrooms in a forest, commercial mycelium grows quickly – from visible specks to a block the size of an encyclopaedia (though much lighter) within a week. Incredible stuff.

When foraging, you must be certain of the mushrooms you choose to handle. Take a course, do some research online, borrow a book from a library, join a group or forage with a knowledgeable friend. Never eat any mushrooms unless you are 100 per cent sure that you've identified it correctly — if in doubt, toss it out (or don't pick it in the first place). As with any foraging or time spent in nature, leave little trace and allow the natural environment to thrive. Never take more mushrooms than you need, and leave the roots of the mushroom behind to ensure future growth.

WHEN TO FORAGE

All mushrooms, including edible ones, need shade and moisture to grow. They will most likely appear in the days after heavy rainfall, with the support of plenty of sun and temperatures of 15–23°C (59–74°F). In most places, autumn is the optimal time of year to go mushrooming. As for time of day, early morning is best as they grow overnight, and it's a popular early morning activity among in-the-know foragers.

WHERE TO FORAGE

Mushrooms typically appear above ground, either from the soil or on its food source — often wood. A good place to look for edible mushrooms is in your nearest pine forest or near a river where there are fallen trees. This is because edible mushrooms thrive in the forest floors that surround pine trees, as the fallen needles create a perfectly insulated, temperature-controlled ground soil where they can grow. If you don't have a pine forest nearby, try a river where the water can support the growth of mushrooms on fallen, decaying branches and trees.

WHAT TO LOOK FOR

Here are three types of common edible mushrooms you can forage for.

137

SAFFRON MILK CAP
Lactarius deliciosus

This mushroom is a distinctive pinkish-peach or orange colour that will help you locate them. Usually between 5–20cm (2–8in) in diameter, saffron milk caps are concave in the centre with edges that tend to roll inwards. The cap also features orange to red concentric circles. Underneath, the orange gills are quite pronounced. The stem is usually 3–6cm (about 1–2.5in) long and up to 3cm (about 1in) wide, and bulging and cylindrical in shape. It often has quite distinctive darker orange pits on the stem. The mushroom has a pith in the centre of the stem, and as the mushroom ages this pith reduces, meaning the stem becomes hollow.

SLIPPERY JACK
Suillus luteus

This mushroom has a slimy, light to dark brown appearance on top that is entirely smooth and shiny, even when dry. It is a broad mushroom with a conical shape that can grow as big as 13cm (5in) in diameter. Underneath, the mushroom has a yellowish sponge-like look, with small holes and a stout, white stem that can be as much as 10cm (4in) tall and 3cm (about 1in) thick. It will likely have small dots near the top. Slippery jacks bear a distinctive membranous ring on the underside that is tinged brown to violet.

CHANTERELLES
Cantharellus cibarius

Chanterelles are yellow-orange in colour, making them relatively easy to spot. The cap is flat in the middle and reaches upwards in a funnel shape with curled edges. On the inside, the flesh is white and firm, and often smells of apricots or pumpkin. They don't have true gills but instead have rounded ridges or folds that run down the stem. Chanterelles are commonly found in old-growth forests near hardwood trees, such as beech, oak, maple, birch and poplar, or conifers, such as pine or hemlock.

HOW TO FORAGE

It might take you some time to spot a mushroom. They can be hidden, so simply enjoy walking in the pine forest for a time, letting your eyes adjust to the predominantly brown landscape around you. Notice the different shades of brown. Observe the textures of the forest, too. Is it wet or dry? Smooth or rough? Shiny or dull? Mushrooms most often grow near tree bases and fallen branches, so pay attention to those areas. The orange colours of saffron milk caps and chanterelles are a beacon for recognition, while the slippery jacks' warm brown and shiny tops help them stand out. Gently moving pine needles aside can help you find them, as they're often nestled deep below layers of debris. Once you've spotted one, look around the area, as they tend to grow in groups — there will likely be more nearby.

HOW TO HARVEST

Using a sharp knife, cut the mushroom at the stem. Be sure not to harvest the white roots that grow underground (the mycelium) so the mushroom will grow back. Once you have harvested the mushroom, take your brush and gently clean off any dirt or pine needles that are on its surface. It's also a good idea to hold the mushroom over the ground and give it a gentle tap. This will dislodge any spores — by letting them fall to the ground you'll be helping to grow more mushrooms. Once harvested, place your mushrooms in your basket or cardboard box. Only take what you need, and consider not taking mushrooms that are very small so they can grow bigger.

HOW TO PREPARE AND COOK

Only the top of the slippery jack should be eaten. To cook them, peel away the brown skin and remove the spongy bottom — you want to cook just the main flesh of the mushroom. They're best cooked whole — fry them in butter or oil and enjoy as a side dish.

Saffron milk caps are quite firm, meaty mushrooms, and the entire mushroom (including the stalk) can be consumed. Lightly peppery and flavoursome, a simple and classic recipe is to slice them, then fry them in a pan with oil or butter and a little garlic. Serve them hot with a sprinkle of parsley.

Chanterelles are a great addition to soups, pastas and risottos alike, but the peppery and slightly fruity flavour that's made them a favourite with chefs around the world can certainly stand on it's own, too. Simply saute them in butter on a hot pan, adding garlic and/or cream if you want, to serve on it's own, as a side or on toast.

A FINAL WARNING

It can be very difficult to distinguish between toxic and edible varieties of wild mushroom. If you eat the wrong one, there can be major consequences to your health. If you suspect you have consumed poisonous wild mushrooms, don't wait for symptoms to appear; seek medical attention immediately.

For information call:

- Poisons Information Centre (AUS): 13 11 26
- Poison Control (USA): 1800 222 1222
- National Health Service (UK): for non-emergencies contact 111; for emergencies contact 999

RIVER LIFE

141

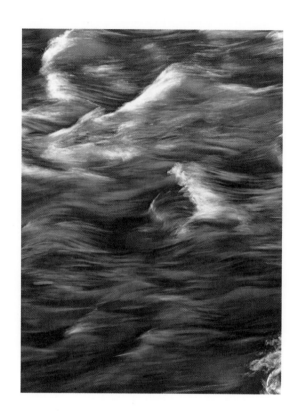

GO WILD SWIMMING

Water has extraordinary power and sustains the Earth and its inhabitants with its hydrating, cleansing and revitalising properties. One of the most effective and enjoyable ways to tap into its benefits is with a wild swim — a dip in a body of natural water, like a river.

Rivers are wide, ribbon-like bodies of water that flow downhill from the force of gravity. They can be deep or shallow enough for a person to wade across, and fast-flowing, slow-moving and anything in between. Starting high in mountains and hills, streams form from the runoff of rain and snow. Droplets become pools, then trickles, then gurgles and babbles that gather momentum and flow downhill. They grow then join together and grow some more, forming mighty rivers that journey towards the ocean. Once at the ocean, liquid water evaporates into water vapour, condenses and forms clouds, eventually precipitating (massing into a substance and falling) back to Earth in the form of rain and snow. This is the water cycle.

Whatever the season, seek out a river and admire its might before taking the plunge. Say yes to its invitation to explore new and invigorating sensations. Use all your senses (*see* page 4). Watch as the light dances across its surface. Listen as the water moves along the path of least resistance and snakes across earth. Witness how wildlife (*see* page 128), birds (*see* page 160) and insects are energised as they interact with the water and each other. Try these tips for your own wild swimming adventure.

FIND YOUR RIVER

Human communities have always gravitated towards sources of fresh water. It is essential for our wellbeing — for example for drinking, washing, cooking, transport, agriculture and energy — and our villages, towns and cities have grown and evolved around it. So, you shouldn't have too far to go to find your own mighty river. It's always best to journey upriver to swim, as the water will be cleaner. You might like to make your wild swim a microadventure (*see* page 100), the cooling reward after a hike (*see* page 110) or the site of a camping

experience (*see* page 118). Most rivers have established swimming spots that can be located with a bit of research. The best places are calm, pool-like spots that have evolved as fast-flowing rapids have carved out pools, or 'waterholes', over time — a calm and relatively still respite where the river water pools and gathers momentum before flowing on.

EQUIPMENT (AND CLOTHING) OPTIONAL

Wild swimming is one activity that doesn't require much equipment, if any. The basics might include a wet suit or swimsuit, a towel and some aqua shoes or old sneakers. If you prefer to skinny dip, make sure you have something warm to put on afterwards to help your body adjust to the changes in temperature.

WATCH HOW THE RIVER WORKS

Embracing your wild side isn't about being reckless. Before you take the plunge, be aware of your surroundings. Check the depth of the water using a stick or walking pole, and be mindful of the strength and direction of the current. Watch how the river works. Where is the water flowing to and from? Are there any bubbling rapids — they are likely to be flowing over and around rocks and fallen trees, so steer clear. Scan the area for obstacles, including fallen branches and other people or boats, and keep an eye out for signs of pollution or algae, such as frothy blooms or scum on the surface of the water. Be aware, too, that heavy rain and storms will make a river level rise and sometimes even make it change its course. Do not go wild swimming in a river during or after heavy rain or storms.

IMMERSE YOURSELF

Will you inch your way into the water, run in screaming a wild release or jump from a rock or riverbank? Choose between the exquisite feeling of slowly immersing yourself in the water or the adrenaline hit of literally taking the plunge. Let go of your daily worries as you immerse your body in the cool, fresh water of a river, pond or stream. Relax as the water washes over you and helps you reconnect with your body. Enjoy the sense of weightlessness. Float. Breathe. Sink

under the surface and enjoy a moment of complete immersion and weightlessness.

Tune in to the feeling of your skin tingling and flushing with fresh blood as the benefits of cold-water swimming (*see* page 178) kick in, such as improved circulation and a strengthened immune system and libido. Be aware that spending too long in very cold water increases the risk of hypothermia. Uncontrollable shivering is one of the first signs to look out for. If you want to be able to spend more time in cold water, wear a wetsuit. Otherwise, take care to only stay in very cold water for a short time.

MULTIPLY YOUR JOY

Many cultures around the world are huge proponents of wild swimming, including Nordic countries and Japan. They take the plunge all year round and even alternate dipping into cold water and then a hot spring or sauna to really get the blood flowing and reap the benefits. Of course, you can try wild swimming in any natural body of water where it is safe to do so. In addition to rivers, you might like to explore wild swimming in lakes, ponds, streams and the ocean (*see* page 176). A Swedish proverb says shared joy is double joy, so why not invite a friend or two along?

PADDLE
A CANOE

Humans have been making canoes to hunt, fish and explore for millennia. Learn a few simple terms and techniques, and you'll soon be paddling up and down rivers, seeing the world from an entirely new perspective and connecting with life in and on the water.

Canoes have been used by many different cultures around the world for millennia, and they have played an important role in human civilisation as a means of exploration, hunting and trade. The oldest known canoe was discovered in the Netherlands and dates back to somewhere between 8200 and 7600 BC. Canoes were originally carved from whole tree trunks or large chunks of wood — so-called dugout canoes — and some cultures developed canoes made from bark or skin fitted around a wooden frame. Today canoes are often made from lightweight fiberglass, but the shape — a long narrow vessel with a curved bottom and pointed up ends — remains relatively unchanged.

Seeing the world go by while floating along a river can be as relaxing or adventurous as you want, and you can plan it to suit your needs and your fitness level. If you're new to canoeing, try to partner up with someone who's experienced and follow the tips below.

PLAN YOUR PADDLE

Research canoeing spots in your local area. It's a good idea to start off small and just paddle for a few hours or spend an afternoon exploring a short stretch of river or an area with a network of rivers. Some canoe hire companies offer pick-up services down river, meaning you don't have to paddle against the current. Once you're more experienced and have built up your paddling fitness, you might like to make a weekend of it — perhaps to travel through a region or from one town to another by river and camp along the way.

If you're daytripping, pack a snack or lunch you can enjoy on the riverbank along the way. Do your research to see if there's anything worth exploring too, such as waterfalls, caves or local wildlife (*see* page 128).

Pack essentials and a change of clothes in a dry bag. If you're camping, pack as you would for any ordinary camping trip (*see* page 118), but pack your kit into waterproof barrels — many canoe hire companies will provide these. As with any intrepid adventure, be sure to tell someone where you're going and when you'll be back.

FAMILIARISE YOURSELF WITH THE CANOE

Canoes are usually symmetrical, with a seat in the front (the bow) and a seat in the rear (the stern, or aft). Each end is designed to pivot around the centre. If you sit in the bow, you'll mainly be responsible for maintaining forward momentum. If you're in the stern, you'll be in charge of steering the canoe in the right direction (and might be the one giving more verbal instructions). Then there's port side, which is the left side as you face the bow, and starboard (the right).

The paddles themselves are used to steer the canoe and have a flat blade designed to cut through the water. Most canoes are designed to seat two people, so ideally this is something you do with a friend or as a group. When there are two active paddlers, it's called tandem paddling. If you do end up paddling a two-person canoe by yourself, kneel between the two seats or sit in the stern.

PUSH OFF AND ENJOY THE RIVER

Check the current and scan the river for any obstacles before you push off, and always wear a life jacket. Once you've pushed off, stay close to the water's edge and take regular breaks. Start off slow. This allows you to get a feel for being in the canoe, practise your paddling strokes and find a good rhythm. You may find yourself tiring quickly from using muscles you may not have used in a while and from all the energy you spend concentrating and learning. If you encounter other canoes or vessels, follow boating rules and stay on the right side of the river. Going canoeing is all about having fun in the great outdoors. Breathe in the fresh air, bask in the sunlight and enjoy getting up close to the river and its wildlife.

If you veer off course, stop, pause and reassess. Use your compass and map (*see* page 114) if you need to reorient yourself, then slowly turn the canoe in the direction you want to go. Once you're back on dry land, pull the canoe all the way out of the water and secure it so it's ready for its next adventure.

MASTER THE BASIC STROKES

Paddling can appear effortless, but there's skill behind every stroke. These basic strokes will help you stay on course and make your paddling adventure an enjoyable one. With a bit of practise, you'll eventually be able to paddle further and faster.

Forward stroke — this is the most common stroke. Place the paddle into the water in front of you, with the blade perpendicular to the boat, and pull the blade back towards the stern. Work on the opposite side of your partner, or alternate sides often if you're paddling solo.

Backward stroke — this stroke is like putting on the canoe's brakes. It's the opposite of the forward stroke, as you put the paddle into the water behind you and drag it forward toward the bow. You can do a 'hard turn' — spinning the canoe

around to go in the opposite direction — if one paddler uses the forward stroke on one side while the other uses the backward stroke on the other side.

Draw stroke — this is more commonly used in fast moving water when you need to move sideways to avoid an obstacle. Keeping the paddles parallel to the boat, both paddlers reach their paddles out on the same side in line with their bodies, then draw their paddle back through the water towards the boat.

These additional strokes are used by the paddler sitting in the stern to navigate and control the canoe:

Pry stroke — this stroke turns the canoe to the side of your paddle. With the blade parallel to the canoe, place the paddle in the water and reach as far behind you as you can, then turn the blade forward at a 45-degree angle.

Sweep stroke — this stroke turns the canoe towards the opposite side of your paddle. With the blade perpendicular to the canoe, place the paddle in the water next to you and and then swing it backwards in a full 90 degree motion, towards the stern.

J stroke — this is a combination of a forward stroke and a pry stroke, and is so-called because you create a J-shape with the paddle. With the blade perpendicular to the canoe, place the paddle into the water in front of you and drag it back towards the stern. Once it's behind you turn the blade so its parallel to the canoe and then move it forward at a 45-degree angle.

DIG
FOR CLAY

Humans have been finding and digging for clay to
shape into practical and aesthetic ceramics for thousands,
even millions, of years. Digging for and working with clay
is a simple and extremely satisfying practice and a wonderful
excuse to get some dirt between your toes.

GATHER

PENKNIFE

BUCKET

SHOVEL OR TROWEL

TARPS OR CLEAN PLASTIC SHEETING (IDEALLY REPURPOSED)

HAMMER

WATER

SIEVE

BOARD OR TABLE TOP

ROLLING PIN (OPTIONAL)

PLASTIC ZIP LOCK BAGS

Clay is a fine-grained, highly malleable natural rock or soil material that becomes hard when dried or fired. It is shaped into bricks, vessels, pottery and other craft and art pieces. All clay is different. Some of the variables that form clay are where it comes from; what types of rocks, soils, minerals and oxides have come together over the years to form it; and how it has been collected, prepared and stored.

FINDING CLAY

Clay can be found on the edges of lakes, rivers, creeks and streams — particularly in the lower parts or edges where the water is calm and still — and in dry river and creek beds. It can also be found where road construction crews and builders have cleared away the topsoil. It can be found both wet and dry, and its colour can range from white to dull grey to brown or a deep orange-red, depending on its mineral content.

When you go looking for clay, ask permission if you want to enter private land. Be careful around waterways, and never dig for clay in environmentally protected, polluted or unstable areas. Check with the local council to ensure it's okay to dig for clay in your area, and make sure you're not putting yourself in physical danger when you dig.

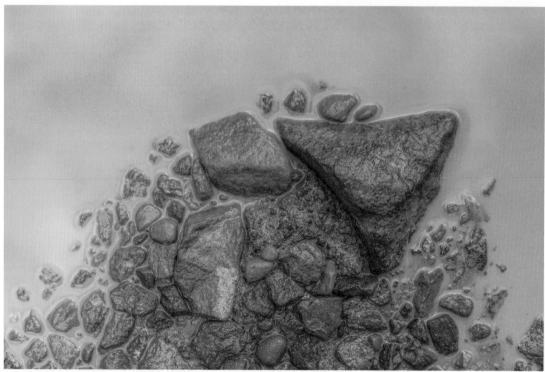

HOW TO RECOGNISE AND DIG FOR CLAY

In its dry state, clay often looks like dirt or rocks, and in its wet state, it looks like mud. If you find dry lumps that you think might be clay, take a chunk and scrape it with your penknife. If it's clay, the fine particles will crumble off. Scrape some into a small pile and dampen it with water to see if it dissolves — if it does, you've found clay.

In a wet area, clear and dig beneath layers of leaves, sand, stones and humus. You'll know you're at or near clay when the mud or soil becomes fine and grainy. Test it by taking a small lump and working it into a ball with your fingers. Roll it into a 'ribbon', then coil it around your finger. If it stays together and feels smooth and pliable, you've found clay. Use your trowel or shovel to gather what you need into your bucket, taking care to avoid stones, twigs and loose topsoil.

PREPARE THE CLAY FOR USE

If the clay is clean and with good plasticity (use the 'ribbon' method described to test it), you'll be able to use it right away, but often, found clay needs to be processed.

Begin by spreading out your haul and letting it dry — note that this could take up to a week. It's best to use a tarp or repurposed plastic for this task, as it will become dirty. Do this indoors or under cover if you can — you don't want the wind blowing things into it! When the clay has dried completely, use a hammer to break it up into pea-sized pieces. If it's already dry, you can get started with the next step straight away.

Fill a bucket with as much water as you have clay, sprinkle the clay into the water and stir. Add more water to make a liquid mass, then let it sit for at least a few hours.

Stir the mixture well, then strain it into another bucket through a sieve or flyscreen, adding water to keep the mixture moving through the sieve if you need to. Leave the sieved clay to settle in the bucket, then pour off any extra water. Repeat this process until the clay is mud-like and free of any foreign objects. Use a trowel to spread it out on a board and make a 'slab' — an old formica tabletop is perfect for this task. You want your slab to be no less than 6mm (1/4in) thick so it is sturdy enough to use without breaking. When it's stiff enough to roll, knead and fold the clay until it feels pliable (this is called 'wedging'). You might find a rolling pin useful. Now it's time to store it.

STORING YOUR CLAY

Separate the wedged clay into workable chunks. Wrap each chunk tightly in several layers of plastic, and put it in an airtight zip lock bag or similar and tightly close the bag. It can be kept this way for months, even years.

MAKE
PINCH POTS

Nature is rarely symmetrical, ordered or tidy — and neither are these handmade clay pinch pots. They're deliberately textured and uneven, and are just the thing for planting succulents, housing stone collections and whatever else you need a little nature-inspired treasure trove for.

GATHER

CLAY (*SEE* PAGE 152)

WATER

ACRYLIC PAINT (OPTIONAL)

PAINTBRUSHES (OPTIONAL)

VARNISH (OPTIONAL)

SHAPE YOUR PINCH POT

Take a wedge of clay and begin by kneading and warming it. Take your time and get to know the clay. Is it dry and crumbly or wet and pliable? You want it to be wet (but not too wet), so if it's dry, add a little water. If it's too wet, try draining off some of the moisture by leaving it in a warm place for the moisture to evaporate, or add some dry clay and work it through.

Enjoy working the clay. Push it, knead it, smack it on the bench. Take your time. When the clay is warm, free of air pockets and has good plasticity (the potter's term for clay that is flexible and good to work with), roll it into a ball with the desired size of your pinch pot in mind.

Push your thumb down into the centre of the ball of clay and create a deep indent. Work through the indent until it is around 1cm (1/2in) from the bottom of the clay ball, then use your thumb and index finger to pinch and press the clay outwards and upwards. With each movement of your fingers, your pot should begin to take shape. Turn it as you pinch to maintain a (relatively) even thickness in the walls and overall shape of the pot.

Take your time to work the pot into a shape that appeals to you, then flatten the bottom by carefully pressing it against a table or a flat work surface. You might want to create small feet for your pot, or you can leave it flat.

Pay attention to the lip of the pot; it doesn't have to be perfect but don't let it get too thin, as this is the part that will probably weather the most wear and tear.

DECORATE YOUR WORK

Use your fingers to smooth out the surface of the pot, then get creative. Household items like spoons, knives and toothpicks, and foraged items like shells, sticks and twigs all make good decorating tools. Potters use all sorts of tools to achieve finished effects on their creations — brass hole cutters, bevel cutters, ribs, pin tools and knives. One of the lovely things about working with clay is that you can always rework it, so don't be afraid to experiment. Try pressing the end of a pencil into the clay to create pockmarks, running a pointy twig through the clay to create patterns or pressing a decorating tool into the clay to make an imprint (*see* page 90 for more on printing with leaves).

DRYING AND FIRING YOUR CREATION

When you're happy with your pinch pot, place it somewhere warm, like a windowsill, for a few days and let it dry. Fire it in a kiln if you can (perhaps take it to your local ceramic workshop) or try a home firing method (*see* page 158). Otherwise, finish it in a way that appeals to you, such as using fine sandpaper to smooth the surface and edges, decorating it with acrylic paint, and if you want a glossy finish, a coat of varnish, too.

MAKE A FIRE PIT TO FIRE YOUR CLAY IN

Firing clay in a pit fire is one of the oldest known methods for firing pottery. Provided you're permitted to do this in your area, it's perfect for trying at home. For the best result, make sure your pots are totally dry before trying to fire them.

GATHER

SPADE

CARDBOARD

SAWDUST

OLD PAPER

DRY KINDLING OR SMALL PIECES OF WOOD

COPPER (OPTIONAL)

SALT (OPTIONAL)

LIGHTER OR MATCHES

WIRE BRUSH

BUCKET OF WATER

BEESWAX OR NATURAL SHOE POLISH

METHOD

1. You'll begin by identifying a place to dig your pit and clearing it of leaves and braches. The hole needs to be big enough for you to be able to place your clay pots in it. They shouldn't be touching and there needs to be a bit of space around them. It might help to lay them on the ground and mark out the digging area around them. You could do this by scraping its outline in the dirt with a stick or laying a piece of string or cordage (*see* page 164) on the ground to mark its perimeter. Keep a bucket of water nearby in case of emergency.

2. Once you've worked out how big the hole needs to be, take your spade and dig out the soil. The hole should be three times deeper than the highest pot you're firing.

3. Feel the soil. If it's damp, insulate your pit by lining it with cardboard.

4. Fill the bottom of the pit with a layer of sawdust about 12cm (5in) deep.

5. Now place your pots on top of the sawdust. Take note of the positions they're in, as they may come out looking quite different depending on where they're placed and you might want to be able to replicate, experiment or adjust next time. You can also experiment with adding copper and salt around your pots to produce colour flashes in the finished pieces.

6. Next, place layers of sawdust, paper and dry wood around your pots. You want to have enough of these materials to keep the fire burning for an hour or so. Keep in mind that sawdust burns quite slowly.

7. Light your fire from the top and allow it to burn out completely, which should take about an hour depending on how much sawdust you used. To contain the heat and help the process, you can cover the pit with a piece of metal. Once the fire has burned itself out, leave it until it's cool enough to touch. This can take several hours.

8. When the pit has cooled, you can dig up the fired pots. They'll be blackened and sooty, so it's time to gently clean them by brushing them with a wire brush and washing them with water. Leave them to dry, then rub with a clear wax, like beeswax or natural shoe polish, or paint them.

Safety note: take care not to put food in vessels that have not been glazed with a food-safe glaze. Any pieces fired in a fire pit will be porous, meaning they cannot be used for liquids.

159

OBSERVE
BIRDS

Birds flock to rivers to find food and water, nest, mate, play and bathe. These fascinating and ancient creatures are descended from dinosaurs and have captivated cultures around the world for thousands of years. Watch and listen carefully, and you'll begin to unlock and understand their melodic language.

Birds have been observed by cultures around the world for thousands of years; they've inspired songs and dances, informed aeronautical technology and play an essential role in nature. Not only are they nature's alarm clock, using their song to declare the dawning of each new day, they play a vital role in our ecosystem as pollinators and alert other animals of danger.

Birdwatching is a popular activity across the world. It is a simple and beautiful way to tune into nature and connect with your wild side. A birder, or twitcher, is the common term for a birdwatcher — it's different from ornithology, which is the branch of zoology devoted to studying birds. Birdwatching, or simply birding, can be done by anyone — kind of like citizen science for bird lovers. Practicing being a birder requires you to listen and concentrate deeply and use all your senses (*see* page 4) as you seek out and study our avian friends. Bird language is universal and birds are everywhere, so once you learn this skill you can apply it wherever you go.

GET STARTED

You only need to look out the window or venture out of your front door to start birdwatching. Once you've enjoyed getting to know your neighbourhood birds, you might like to seek out areas where one habitat changes to another — like the places where land becomes water. Birds and other wildlife are drawn to rivers and lakes for food, bathing opportunities, nesting spots and social interaction, so they're a great place to start looking for new species. You can also research ahead of time. A field guide from your local library, council or conservation group can help with bird identification.

You can observe birds with your naked eye. You might spot a few 'nottabirds' or 'pseudobirds' — something that looks like a bird from a distance but ends up being something else. If you start to really enjoy the experience and want to see more, or better, consider investing in a pair of binoculars ('bins' in birder slang).

PLAN YOUR TIME

Consider the best time of day to go. Most birds are diurnal (daytime) creatures. They're extremely active at dawn, busy feeding and preening in the morning, restful from noon through the afternoon before becoming active again in the late afternoon and evening before dusk, when they nest and settle down for the night. The exception to this rule is ducks and swans, which can be spotted going about their business any time of day. Nocturnal birds like owls and nightjars rest during the day and become active as night descends.

LOOK A LITTLE CLOSER

Once you're at your location, find a comfortable spot and try to remain calm and still. To begin with, simply pause and tune in to the birdlife around you. Observe them. Notice their appearance, sounds and behaviours. Begin to appreciate how each type of bird has its own distinct rhythm of movement. Remember, they'll also be observing you. Watch and listen to how they react when you move. Remember to be careful and respectful of their boundaries — you are in their territory. At certain times of year, especially when baby birds are around, some birds become extremely protective of their young and may swoop and squawk to stop you from approaching.

161

How many birds can you identify by looking at them? Or by listening to them? You can probably identify more birds than you realise. There are likely to be many common birds around your home, and as you explore a new area you'll probably see some birds that don't look familiar. Depending on where you live and where in the world you go birding, you may come across everything from herons and hummingbirds to pelicans and penguins. You may even get lucky and see a flock of flamingos, the elusive toucan or majestic birds of prey soar across the sky.

Birders identify birds by looking at their shape, size, markings, posture, behaviour and colours, so look for any distinguishing features – referred to by birders as field marks – that might help you narrow down its type. Does it have a brightly coloured spot or pattern on its wings? An unusually shaped beak, large talons or distinctive tail feathers? Take your nature journal (*see* page 82) and jot down the features you notice, or take some photos you can study later. This will help hone your observational skills and help to keep a record of your adventure.

LOOK IT UP

Birdwatching has its own unique terminology and language, and avid birdwatchers often keep a list of the species they've spotted and those they'd like to see. Using a field guide specific to the area you're exploring can help you identify the different species of birds more easily.

TUNE IN

Birds have their own distinct sounds and signals, but how do you distinguish the meaning of a squawk, hoot, chirp, cheep or tweet? It often comes down to the pitch and tempo. With practise and patience, you'll develop an ear for identifying common sounds or voices of birds. These can include:

Songs — melodious tweets and whistles that vary across species. Birds use these songs during courtship and as territorial signals.

Companion calls — friendly, soft and rhythmic sounds, often quietly shared during feeding.

Territorial aggression — loud and aggressive calls, often combined with aggressive behaviour as they warn off other birds.

Juvenile begging — urgent calls of hunger by young birds demanding to be fed.

Alarms — loud warning sounds that indicate predators or threats within the landscape. These vary even within species to communicate different types of danger.

EXPERIENCE THE DAWN CHORUS

While many of us are still soundly asleep, nature wakes up and celebrates life with joyful exuberance. Birds unite in song to greet the new day with a special symphony known as the dawn chorus.

Why not join them? You might like to completely immerse yourself in the experience by camping near a river overnight (*see* page 118) and waking up with the light and sounds of nature, or you can stay at home and set your alarm to wake before dawn. Experience the quiet stillness and calm as night transitions into day. Venture outside and watch as light and colour fill the sky. Settle in and be enthralled by the morning song of birds.

163

MAKE STRING AND CORDAGE

Making string, cordage and rope from plant fibres is an ancient art. This simple two ply cordage is a pleasure to make, creates tight and even string of very high quality and can be used for all sorts of projects, from jewellery making and gift wrapping to basket making, net weaving and bushcraft adventures.

GATHER

PLANT FIBRES

WATER

Plant fibres can be extracted from myriad plants and plant parts, such as leaves, stems, seeds and husks. These fibres provide structure for plants and have moisture-retentive properties that help them in their survival. Simply put, the plant fibres are the 'stringy bits' you can peel off, and they can often be divided into smaller and smaller strips, which is useful to know, as the width of these strips will affect the size of your string.

The best material to use will depend on what's available in your area. The easiest fibres to work with are long and even, and using fibres of similar thickness is key to making good, strong cord. Good options include stinging nettles, reeds, rushes, grasses and bark — even animal hair can be used. Rushes, reeds and grasses are easy to begin with, as you can strip the fibres straight from the plant. Some types of bark can be stripped and used straight away, too, but it may require a bit of work to strip the bark from the tree trunk — never strip the bark off living trees (*see* page 133 for more information on how to source wood sustainably). Fibres from fresh, green plants may require a bit more work to prepare, and these will likely need to be dried before use, which can take several days.

Different types of fibre will produce different coloured fibres of varying strengths, so experiment with the plants that are available in your area to see what works best for your purpose.

PREPARING YOUR FIBRES

If you have a range of fibres of varying thickness, group them together according to thickness, and use them to make separate strings. Of course, all strands vary and thin out at some point, but don't worry too much about this; you'll be adding in new fibres when you weave the strands together.

Dampen your fibres with water to make them supple and easier to grip. Some fibres are suited for soaking, others for dunking and others for simply having water run over them with wet fingers. Experiment with a sample fibre to work out what suits your fibres best.

MAKING AN EYE

Always begin by making an 'eye'. To do this, take up two lengths of fibre and stagger them so that half of them overlap, then fold them in half and adjust where the bend sits, making sure the ends are uneven. This is so when the ends run short later they don't end (and therefore need to have new fibre woven in) at the same point in the cord.

Now locate the area where the two lengths are overlapping. Using your thumbs and index fingers, pinch the fibres about 2.5cm (1in) apart, and twist them in opposite directions. As tension builds the fibres will naturally kink to form a small loop — the eye; this will be the end of your cord. Pinch the loop between the thumb and forefinger of your nondominant hand — you will move this hand along the cord as you weave, and your other hand will do all the twisting.

WEAVING THE CORD

Holding the eye in one hand, grab the strand that is furthest away from you with your other hand and twist it tightly. Maintaining the tautness in the twist you've created, bring the strand forward and over the top of the strand that is closest to you so they swap places. Pinch the twist you've just created with one hand, then repeat the process of taking the strand that is furthest away from you, twisting it and holding it taut, then bringing it up and over the front strand with your other hand. This process can also be done in reverse — taking the strand closest to you and moving it away and under after twisting it — so experiment to see what feels most natural to you.

REPLACING FIBRES

When one of the strands becomes thinner than the other, you need to add in a new strand of fibre. Take a new piece of fibre and add it to the end of the thinning strand, making sure there's an overlap and that the thickness stays as even as possible throughout. Pinch it into place, then carry on twisting and rolling your cord (and adding in new fibres, as needed) until you have the length of cord you desire.

You can use your cord while camping or hiking, or turn it into nifty string bags (*see* page 168).

WEAVE A STRING BAG

Archaeologists have discovered fragments of bags and nets made with knotless netting in ancient civilisations from Scandinavia to the USA. Learn how to turn simple plant-fibre cordage into netting by creating your very own string bag — that might even stand the test of time.

GATHER

PLANT-FIBRE CORDAGE (*SEE* PAGE 164)

OR PREMADE STRING

BLUNT TAPESTRY NEEDLE

SCISSORS

Once you've mastered making your own cordage (*see* page 164), follow these simple steps to turn your string into something that will give you pleasure every time you use it: a string bag.

METHOD

1. Find a comfortable sitting position, then take several metres of string or cordage and wrap it twice around your thigh, or around both legs if you want to make a large bag. Tie a knot at one end of the string. This will be the rim of your bag.

Find the other end of string and thread it through a blunt tapestry needle.

2. Point your needle over the rim and pull down on the end until you have a small loop under the rim. You can make this loop as big or small as you'd like — this will determine the size of the gaps in your bag. For a neat look, it's important to keep your loops consistent in size and keep checking the shape of your bag.

3. Then, point the string back through the front of the nearest side of the loop and pull it tight so you have created a twist.

Repeat this stitch along the row, turning it around your leg as you go until you have loops all the way along the string as it circles your legs.

The first stitch in the second row is created by pointing your needle through the lowest part of the loop in the row above.

4. Carry on stitching rows of loops in this way until the bag is as long as you want it to be.

When you are finished, slip the bag down your leg.

5. For a square bottom, simply lie the bag flat and do a row of running stitch in and out of the loops joining them together.

For a round bottom, skip stitches in each row until the bottom is just one tight loop, then stitch the final row together.

6. Finish with a knot and trim any messy bits with scissors.

To make a simple handle, run a piece of cordage under the rim and twist or plait it together and tie it off on the other side.

169

PAINT
STONES

Painting stones is a fun little project to do at home, and they can be used as paperweights, plant decorations and children's toys, or simply framed as beautiful artworks.

GATHER

STONES

ACRYLIC PAINT OR INK

SMALL PAINTBRUSH

ACRYLIC MATT UV VARNISH

LARGE WATERCOLOUR BRUSH

You can keep an eye out for stones anywhere, but good places to look are at the beach and by rivers. Choose stones that are very smooth and beautifully rounded. Not only are they more pleasing to look at and hold, but painting a smooth stone is much easier than painting a bumpy, uneven one.

When it comes to painting stones, the only limit is your imagination. You can draw inspiration from nature and paint anything from a tree to patterns found on a leaf. If you're new to this type of painting, start with simple patterns and work your way up to more complex designs as you become used to the feel of the brush and ink. Don't feel you have to stick to using just white paint either — you can paint a stone completely black first, then add the design on top in white for a more dramatic, graphic look or play around with different colours. There are no rules, so just have fun.

Use acrylic paint or acrylic ink — this free-flowing ink makes it easier to paint fine details and dries to a smooth, matt finish. You'll need a small brush with a fine point. Try experimenting with different combinations of stones, mixing various shapes, colours and designs to create unique and striking collections. Use a varnish that works on the sort of paint you have used, applying it with a larger, soft watercolour brush for an even coat. A matt UV varnish works best, as it doesn't interfere with the natural beauty of the stone.

METHOD

1. Wash the stones in warm, soapy water, rinse well and leave them to air-dry. When the stones are dry, they'll be ready to paint on.

2. Paint your stones however you wish.

3. Leave the ink to dry overnight.

4. Give the stones a coat of varnish to protect the design and bring out the depth of colour in the stone itself.

5. When the varnish is dry, your stones will be ready to display, either alone or as part of a collection.

171

COAST
LIFE

173

SWIM IN
THE OCEAN

The vast and mysterious ocean is truly awe-inspiring. Its twin therapeutic benefits of cold water and salt immersion will leave you feeling invigorated, energised and cleansed. Embrace the natural high and feeling of euphoria that comes from wild ocean swimming.

The ocean is a massive body of saltwater that covers about 71 per cent of the Earth's surface. Oceanographers and the countries of the world divide the ocean into five distinct bodies: the Pacific, Atlantic, Indian, Southern and Arctic oceans. Then there are the seas — more than 50 of them, which we also include in our cultural thinking about the oceans. Seas are smaller than oceans and are partially enclosed by land. In truth, they are all one vast body of water that rolls around the Earth: the ocean.

Scientists estimate that 97 per cent of the world's water is in the ocean. This means it has considerable impact on weather, temperature and the food supply of humans and other organisms, and it is a vital part of the water cycle. However, despite its size and vital role in life on Earth, the ocean remains a mystery. More than 80 per cent of the ocean remains unmapped and unexplored by humans.

Standing on the coastline — surrounded by saltwater and with the sky stretching out above and before you — can be restorative and invigorating. The ocean is powerful and unpredictable, sometimes still and calm, other times intensely wild. Take some time to slow down and tune into your senses (*see* page 4). Breathe in the fresh salty air. Scan the horizon. Watch the waves — are they big and stormy or calm and gentle? Is the tide coming in or out (*see* page 188)? Observe the wildlife (*see* page 128) and birds (*see* page 160) that make their home in and alongside the sand and sea.

Humans have been ocean swimming for thousands of years. Its combination of mineral salts and cold water make for excellent cardiovascular exercise, boosts your immune system, cleanses your skin and reduces inflammation. Try these tips to make the most of your next ocean swim.

BE PREPARED

Wherever you are, always prepare carefully for an ocean swim. The ocean is captivating but can also be dangerous. It's more challenging to swim in the ocean than pools, lakes and rivers because you must contend with waves, the tide, the changing landscape of the beach and currents that may not be visible on the surface but can pull strongly underneath.

Learn to read the tides and check for rip currents that can pull you out to sea (*see* page 188). It is also important to watch out for harmful sea creatures that can sting or bite and check the water quality before you go in. If there has been a recent storm or heavy rainfall, the water may be contaminated from the run-off. Avoid areas with an outfall nearby, which is where a river, drain or sewer empties into the sea.

Always swim with others. Choose patrolled beaches, and if there are flags, stay between them. If the water is very cold, you may be at risk of developing hypothermia, so wear suitable gear (see the next tip) and monitor for symptoms like excessive shivering.

SUIT UP!

You can wear a swimsuit for ocean swimming, but if you're not used to spending time in cold water, it's safest, and possibly more enjoyable, to wear a wetsuit. You should also consider wearing goggles, a swimming cap and even booties and gloves to keep you warm. Remember a towel and some warm clothes to put on afterwards. Sipping a warm drink after a cold swim is also a great way to restore your body temperature, so prepare a thermos of tea or hot chocolate.

177

GO SLOWLY

Take your time and ease into it. You might just start with a dip, where you get into the water for a few minutes and adapt to the temperature. Keep moving! Your body will soon adjust. If you're new to ocean swimming, spend some time swimming in relatively calm waters before taking the plunge and heading further out.

The most suitable stroke for ocean swimming is freestyle (also called front crawl), which can be adapted to the more strategic ocean walker swim stroke (see opposite). If you're just starting out, swim close to the shore at times when the ocean is relatively calm, such as around a neap tide (see page 188) until you have built strength and become accustomed to the pull of the ocean. Experienced ocean swimmers like to head out beyond the waves and then swim parallel to the beach (usually against the current) before drifting back in on the waves when they're done. When you're confident and fit enough to try this, stay safe by picking a landmark to keep an eye on while you swim — perhaps a lighthouse, pier or lifesaver's hut. Don't go too far out and make sure to check your surroundings and your distance from the beach from time to time so you know you're on track.

EMBRACE THE BENEFITS OF COLD WATER

The healing powers of the ocean have long been understood. The ancient Romans developed the practice of 'thalassotherapy', which uses seawater to improve health and wellbeing. More modern proponents claim that regular cold water and ice bath immersion — often in combination with meditative breathing techniques — can help fight modern diseases. In recent years,

cold water swimming and ice bathing groups have surged in popularity. Once you've taken the plunge, you'll instantly experience the benefits of being in cold water. Feel the rush as your brain releases the 'happy hormones' serotonin and dopamine, instantly boosting your mood.

EMBRACE THE BENEFITS OF SALT WATER

It's not just the cold temperature of the water and increased movement of the body (see page 8) that will leave you glowing after your ocean swim. Ocean water has specific properties because of its high levels of minerals. These include sodium (salt), of course, but also other minerals our bodies need, such as calcium, chloride, potassium, sulphate and magnesium, a natural muscle relaxant that helps reduce aches and pains. These minerals are found in significantly higher levels in oceans than in river water. Seawater can also have a healing effect on minor cuts and abrasions and may even improve some skin conditions. Your skin will glow from the combination of the mineral-rich water, while the cold water and exercise will give it a healthy flush and increase your circulation. The sea air itself also tends to be less polluted than the air in large cities. When you breathe in the tiny salt particles in the air, it can strengthen your body's immune system and may even temporarily alleviate respiratory conditions, such as asthma and hay fever.

BASK IN THE AFTERGLOW

As you come out of the ocean after your swim, notice what has shifted within your body and mind. You may find your mind feels more expansive and open. Your body may feel tired yet energised.

HOW TO DO THE OCEAN WALKER SWIM STROKE

Try making these four adjustments to your freestyle stroke to gain more endurance when ocean swimming.

1. Use your core: Instead of using your chest and shoulders to drive your hand and arm into the water, use your core. Imagine turning your hips and using them to propel you through the water.

2. Make your hand enter early: In regular freestyle, your hand enters the water about a forearm's length in front of you, but with ocean walker stroke, you want your hand to enter the water just in front of your head.

3. Extend your arm: In a normal stroke, you'll already be pulling your arm back as you begin to enter the other hand into the water. Instead, keep your arm extended out in front of you until the other hand is about to enter the water, then pull it back.

4. Only pull back to your hips: In regular freestyle you pull your arm back to the level of your thigh, but for ocean walker, you want to pull it back to your hips, which the stroke's creator, record breaking British ocean swimmer Adam Walker, calls the power section.

179

"LIVE IN THE SUNSHINE, SWIM THE SEA, DRINK THE WILD AIR..."

RALPH WALDO EMERSON,
MERLIN'S SONG

WALK
BAREFOOT

Barefoot walking is a simple and easy way to connect with the natural world and it offers some surprising benefits. When you walk barefoot, you 'ground' or 'earth' yourself — meaning you rebalance the energy in your body by aiding a transfer of electrons between you and the Earth. Kick off your shoes and try it yourself.

How long has it been since you took off your shoes and really felt the earth beneath you? Barefoot walking can be done on any of the Earth's natural surfaces where it is safe to do so — in your back garden, a local park, alongside a river and, of course, at the beach.

Connecting to the Earth in this way is sometimes referred to as grounding or earthing. Research, observations and related theories point to the intriguing possibility that the electrons on the Earth's surface are an untapped health resource and consider the Earth a 'global treatment table'. Emerging evidence shows that contact with the Earth may be a simple, natural and profoundly effective environmental strategy against a host of modern ailments, including chronic stress, inflammation, pain, poor sleep and cardiovascular disease. Some researchers even suggested that grounding or earthing the human body could be an essential element in human health, along with exercise (see page 8), sunlight (see page 18), clean air, water and nutritious food. You can 'ground' by wiggling your toes in the sand, pushing your hands into the soil in your garden or taking a moment to lie on your back under a tree.

Walking barefoot sure feels good. Our feet carry our weight day in and day out. Shoes can be supportive and protective, but they can weaken the muscles in our feet, reduce their flexibility and further remove us from the Earth, as most modern shoes are made from insulating rubber or plastic-soled shoes, which do not conduct the flow of electrons.

Walking barefoot awakens the skin on your soles, provides a natural massage for the muscles and gently stretches out the tendons. Next time you're at the beach, try these simple ideas for rejuvenating your feet.

FIND TIME TO 'HEEL'

The beach is a popular and natural choice for walking barefoot. The sand is generally soft and pleasant to walk on, and being near the water's edge and feeling the waves lap over your feet can be soothing and enjoyable. If the beach has smooth pebbles, these can give your soles a deeper, more relaxing massage.

As you walk, really focus on how your feet, ankles and even calves feel. Without shoes, you'll probably feel some muscles and tendons stretching and readjusting. Is the sand hot or cool beneath you? Is it dry so your feet sink into it, or are you closer to the water on firmer ground? Where's the point where you start to sink into the sand? Look back every now and then and observe your footprints in the sand and notice how far you've come. Always keep an eye out for anything sharp or prickly, and avoid areas that are too rocky and hard to walk on.

TRY NATURE'S PEDICURE

Once you've finished walking and your feet are relaxed, why not pamper them a little more? Head down to the water and bathe them in the mineral-rich water of the ocean (see page 176). Gently rub sand onto them as a natural exfoliant to leave the skin fresh and smooth (see page 198) and then let them dry in the warmth of the sun.

FORAGE FOR SEAWEED

From microscopic phytoplankton to giant underwater kelp forests, seaweed is found in oceans across the world. Despite its name, it is not a weed but a type of algae. Abundant in coastal areas, seaweed is a nutritious and delicious addition to your cooking and is easy to forage for.

GATHER

BASKET OR BAG

SLIP-PROOF SHOES

FOLDABLE SHARP KNIFE

Seaweed is the general term for thousands of species of red, brown and green algae that are harvested on a large scale for food and agricultural purposes. These algae provide a habitat for marine life, produce 50 per cent of the Earth's oxygen and have been a staple in the diets of many cuisines around the world — including Japanese, Korean, Irish and Chilean cuisines — for thousands of years.

This widely accessible wild food contains antioxidants, such as iodine, iron and calcium, plus dietary fibre. Seaweed is also popular in cuisines around the world for its unique umami flavour, now known as the fifth taste sensation, alongside salty, sweet, sour and bitter. It adds a savoury, sometimes meaty, and highly irresistible flavour to dishes.

Cultivate your curiosity for new flavours, head to your nearest beach and follow these tips to learn how to forage, cook and enjoy seaweed.

WHEN TO FORAGE

Seaweed availability varies with the seasons. Some species grow year-round, while others are only available in certain months. Find out which types of seaweed are available in your area by researching online, visiting your local library or connecting with local ocean, foraging or wild-food groups.

Before you venture out, it's important to check with local authorities about any restrictions on harvesting seaweed. There may be certain protected species or limits to the amount you can take for personal use.

WHERE TO FORAGE

You can find seaweed at most beaches and coastal areas. Forage in areas with clean, unpolluted water and avoid ocean outfalls, which is where wastewater discharges into the sea.

The easiest seaweed to forage is the kind you'll find washed up on the sand, often referred to as beach cast seaweed. Like all food, fresh is best, so look for recently cast seaweed — it should be wet, rather than dry, and pleasant on the nose. You can look for seaweed in its preferred habitats, including rock pools, boulders and rocky outcrops.

Be mindful of the tides and weather if you are foraging in exposed areas like rocky outcrops. Wear nonslip shoes for added safety, and tell someone where you're going and when you'll be back. To maximise your chances of accessing fresh seaweed, learn to read the tide (*see* page 188) and time your search for when the tide is at least halfway out, as a receding tide exposes the seaweed and gives you time to gather it before the next tide comes in.

HOW TO FORAGE

As with all foraging, be careful to preserve the environment and only take what you need. Only collect pieces of seaweed floating in the water or freshly cast on to the beach. This ensures you won't damage the holdfast, which is a bit like a tree root that helps anchor the seaweed in place. Never yank or cut seaweed from the rock it's anchored to, as this can kill the plants.

185

HOW TO PREPARE AND COOK

Rinse the seaweed in the ocean to remove any grit or other marine life.

At home, rinse it with fresh water. Most seaweed is more palatable to eat dried.

Larger seaweed, such as kelp, can be hung up and dried naturally. Smaller varieties, such as dulse, can be dried in the oven, dehydrator or airing cupboard.

Once the seaweed is dry and crisp, store it in an airtight container. You can eat the pieces on their own or tear them up to add to meals for an umami hit.

TYPES OF SEAWEED TO FORAGE FOR

Most seaweeds are edible; however, some algal blooms can contaminate seaweed, so check for any warnings posted on the beach before you forage.

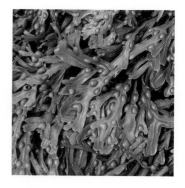

WRACK
Fucus vesiculosus

Known more commonly as bladder wrack, black tang and rockweed, this genus of olive brown seaweed is found on rocky coastlines. It has forked, flattened blades and a prominent midrib, and can be eaten fresh or dried.

DULSE
Palmaria palmata

Featuring long ribbons, this seaweed is found hanging from rocks. It is delicious eaten fresh or dried.

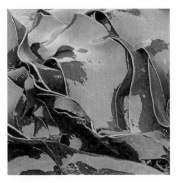

KELP
Laminariales, Alaria esculenta

Kelp is found in temperate and colder waters and includes many of the most well-known edible seaweed, such as wakame, kombu, bull kelp, golden kelp and sugar kelp.

SEA LETTUCE
Ulva lactuca

This common bright-green, lettuce-like seaweed lives on rocks in the intertidal zone. Use it fresh, blanched or dried.

LAVER/NORI
Porphyra umbilicalis

Found clinging to rocks around the high-tide mark, this seaweed resembles cellophane when it's dried. Various species of it are known as laver in Europe, nori in Japan and karengo in Aotearoa (New Zealand). It is possibly the one you're most familiar with, as it is used in sushi.

READ
THE TIDES

Tides are 'long-period' waves that the ocean is drawing back and forth around the planet by the gravitational pull of the moon and sun's monthly and yearly orbits. Learning to read the tides can help us understand more about our incredible planet and its oceans.

Understanding the tides invites you to engage more fully with the timeless and enduring rhythms of nature. It can be almost hypnotic watching the ebb and flow of waves reaching and receding from the shore. The rise and fall of the ocean are akin to breathing. Take time to slow down and tune into your senses (*see* page 4) and appreciate its effortless power.

TYPES OF TIDES

Tides can influence (and be influenced by) the shape of the land and local wind and weather. High and low tide occur when the highest or lowest part of the tide has reached a particular location. The height difference between the two is called the tidal range. At high tide more water covers the shoreline, while at low tide water recedes and reveals more land.

Most coastal areas have two high tides and two low tides every 24 hours, connected to the Earth's rotation. Other tides occur less frequently, reflecting key phases of the moon (*see* page 28). Spring tides (also colloquially named king tides) refer not to the season but to the way the tide 'springs forth' during the new and full moons. Spring tides occur twice each lunar month throughout the year. They bring unusually high water levels and can cause tidal flooding.

Neap tides are tides that also occur twice a month, but they happen when the sun and moon are at right angles to each other. These are moderate tides, where the high tides are a little lower and the low tides are a little higher than average. They occur during the first and third quarters of the moon.

BE ON TIDE TIME

Coastal activities are generally safer and more enjoyable during particular tides. Plan around the tides to choose the best time to head to the beach for a swim or surf, to go fishing or sailing, or even forage for seaweed (*see* page 184). Low tides are ideal for beach walks and foraging. High tides are great for taking the boat out. Surfing, fishing, beach combing and exploring tide pools are more enjoyable between the high and low tides. Avoid ocean swimming (*see* page 176) during spring tides.

READ AND UNDERSTAND WAVES

The easiest way to know whether a tide is coming in or going out is to look for visual clues. This includes looking at the waterline separating the dry and wet sand. Watch the waves for a while to see if they reach the same point. They'll consistently cross the beach face (the part of the beach that is reached by the ocean) if the tide is coming in (approaching high tide) or fail to reach it and recede further away from the land if it's going out (approaching low tide).

Look at other landmarks, such as rocks, boulders, trees and piers, to see at which point they are getting wet.

Close observation of ripples on calmer water can also help you identify the direction of the tide. Ripples pushing towards the shore indicate a high tide.

The presence of debris on the sand, such as seaweed, branches and trash, can also indicate a high tide, as the water brings in and deposits such items.

HOW TO SPOT AND STAY SAFE AROUND RIPS

Rip currents are frequent at most beaches and coastal regions. Learning how to spot them and what to do if you get caught in one is an important and potentially life-saving skill.

Rip currents are strong offshore flows that occur when the water that is pushed to shore by the waves returns back to the ocean. Rips can be deceptive, as they often look like a ribbon of calm water between the waves, but don't be fooled by its calm appearance — they can be very powerful forces of nature. Rip currents are generally no more than 25m (80ft) wide, but there may be several at a given time spaced widely along the shore. They're often present in knee-to-waist-high water.

Before you go in the water, take some time on the shore to access the sea. To spot potential rips, look out for deeper, darker water, fewer breaking waves, ripples on the surface surrounded by smooth waters and anything flowing out to sea, but beware that rips don't always show all of these signs.

If you find yourself in one, stay calm and walk back toward shore against the current once you are in chest-deep water. If you get swept away from shore, swim parallel to the shore instead of towards it until you are beyond the rip's width and can swim or float back to shore with the assistance of the waves that are rolling in.

PROTECT
OUR OCEANS

A healthy ocean means a healthy planet. The home to millions of plants and animals, our ocean absorbs 50 times more carbon dioxide than our atmosphere, provides protein sources for our diet and regulates our climate. Protecting it is vital for the health and wellbeing of all life on Earth.

The ocean helps us breathe, as tiny plant-like organisms that live in the sea called phytoplankton are responsible for at least 50 per cent of the oxygen on Earth. It absorbs and redistributes heat from the sun, regulates rainfall and droughts through its ocean currents and plays a vital role in the water cycle (*see* page 145).

The ocean is also an important source of food and accounts for almost 16 per cent of all animal protein consumed globally. Of course, there's more to seafood than fish, crustaceans and other edible creatures. A range of algae and sea plants (*see* page 184) are also used in cooking.

The ocean is home to incredible biodiversity, and researchers estimate that 91 per cent of species in the ocean still await description. That's mostly due to the vastness of the ocean, which covers around 70 per cent of the planet's surface and is up to 11,000m (36,000ft) deep. The number of yet-to-be-discovered creatures living in the sea could easily run into the millions.

Sadly, the health of our precious and wondrous ocean is under serious threat. Plastic pollution, overfishing and climate change are among the dangers jeopardising our marine environments.

Decades of reliance on cheap and durable plastics has become a particularly costly convenience, and nature is paying the price. An estimated 8 billion kg (17 billion lb) of plastic enters our ocean every year, and there are approximately 5 trillion plastic pieces weighing 250,000 metric tons floating in our oceans.

Consider the impact this has on wildlife. Research indicates that approximately 52 per cent of sea turtles have ingested plastic waste, and by 2050 almost every seabird will have plastic in its stomach. Wildlife will continue to suffer, and our oceans will become increasingly depleted if we don't take the necessary action to reduce our impact on the ocean.

These issues can seem insurmountable, but there is always hope. Just think about the epic, almost two-year long clean-up of Versova Beach in Mumbai, India, which saw volunteers remove more than 12,000 tonnes of plastic and enabled local communities to use it recreationally once again.

Continue to explore and enjoy the ocean but do it respectfully. By remaining connected and committed to our planet, we appreciate it more and understand what we need to do to heal, conserve and preserve it. Do your part to protect the ocean with these tips.

REDUCE YOUR USE OF PLASTIC

Out of all the plastic waste ever generated, only 9 per cent has been recycled, with the remaining 91 per cent ending up in landfills, floating in our oceans or as toxic smoke when burned. Swim against the tide of plastic and say no to plastic packaging.

Around 40 per cent of plastics consumed are single use. Always opt for reusable items. This includes straws, shopping bags, coffee cups, water bottles, cutlery and plates. If you don't have your reusable coffee cup on you, say no to the takeaway lid (or skip the coffee).

Other more environmentally friendly swaps include packing your own lunch or taking your own reusable container when buying takeaway, swapping balloons for blowing bubbles at celebrations and using bamboo or paper cotton swabs instead of plastic ones.

AVOID PRODUCTS THAT HARM

Choose nontoxic chemicals and dispose of toxic ones properly. Oxybenzone, a common ingredient in sunscreens, is particularly damaging to marine life, so look for a marine-friendly alternative.

Don't buy products that may harm endangered or threatened species, such as cosmetics containing shark squalene, souvenirs made of coral or sea turtle shell, and souvenir shells of conchs, nautiluses and other animals. Buying these products supports unsustainable fishing practices.

EAT SUSTAINABLE SEAFOOD

Choosing sustainable seafood helps protect threatened species from overfishing, protects habitats and promotes a balanced ecosystem. Be mindful when planning your next seafood meal and choose:

- Small fish, such as anchovies, herrings and sardines, instead of larger species
- Wild fish, not farmed
- Line-caught fish over trawled or netted catches
- Local fish whenever possible
- Farmed shellfish, including lobster, clams, oysters and crab.

TAKE THREE FOR THE SEA

It is unlikely you will find a pristine beach next time you head to the ocean, so every time you visit the beach, pick up (at least) three pieces of litter to dispose of them properly. If everyone adopted this habit, imagine what a difference it would make.

LEAVE ONLY FOOTPRINTS

Respecting every habitat helps reduce our impact on it. Be sure to take all your litter and trash with you. If you're out at sea, anchor your boat away from coral and sea grasses, and abide by 'no wake' zones. These are areas within which vessels are required to travel at idling speed — slow speed that creates no appreciable wake — to protect marine life.

STAY INFORMED

Read. Listen. Watch. Ongoing awareness, knowledge and education about the health of our ocean can be an important motivator and a key to maintaining your commitment to protect the ocean.

MAKE SOME WAVES

If you see an opportunity to speak up and create change, take it! This might include:

- Asking for a plastic-free alternative at your supermarket or favourite takeaway joint
- Voting for public officials who are committed to protecting our ocean and marine environments
- Joining or supporting local or global marine conservation organisations
- Using your talents or interests to raise awareness — be it through creating art, music or writing — or simply talking about it in your social circles to create a ripple effect.

HARVEST SEA SALT

Salt is a flavour synonymous with the ocean. Spend any time at the beach, and you'll breathe in the ocean's briny fragrance and taste its saltiness on your lips. More pure than processed table salt, sea salt is readily available and offers a unique, local flavour and benefits.

GATHER

CONTAINER

CHEESECLOTH

SAUCEPAN

SHALLOW BAKING TRAYS

CLEAN CLOTH BAG

GRINDER

196

As fresh rainwater washes from the rivers into the sea, it collects salt, or sodium chloride, and other minerals to deposit into the ocean. Salt also comes up from the seafloor through vents and underwater volcanic eruptions. When seawater evaporates it leaves behind dry salt crystals and just like soil influences the flavour of our fruits and vegetables, the different marine and aquatic life in a particular ocean area influences the flavour of sea salt in that area.

Sea salt has been harvested by humans since ancient times. It is sought after for its culinary uses and can also be applied topically in the form of saltwater baths and body scrubs (*see* page 198). Since sea salt is unprocessed, it contains beneficial trace minerals, such as potassium, iron and calcium. Capture some of its salty goodness next time you're at the beach to add a delicious and therapeutic boost to your health at home.

SOURCE THE SEAWATER

To ensure the salt is as pure as possible, source it from clean ocean water. Avoid collecting water near run-off areas (where stormwater or water from heavy rainfall enters the ocean) and areas with an outfall nearby (where a river, drain or sewer empties into the sea), as this water can be contaminated. Water that is too close to the shoreline may also be contaminated

with sand or sunscreen residue, so wade out as far as you safely can or head out in a boat to fill your container, jar or bucket with seawater. You'll need a lot, as roughly 4 litres (1 gallon) yields ½–1 cup of salt.

LET IT SETTLE

Once you bring it home, sit the seawater in a cool place for a few days, so any sediment sinks to the bottom of the vessel it's in. Cover it with a piece of light fabric, like a tea towel or piece of cheesecloth. If you want to speed things up, you can strain the water through several layers of cheesecloth, but be aware you'll be sacrificing some of the salt in the process.

BRING IT TO A BOIL

Scoop, rather than pour, the water into a saucepan so you don't disturb the sediment, and consider pouring it through a sieve lined with cheesecloth if you haven't already done so. Bring the water to the boil and heat it till the water has evaporated, leaving behind the salt. Be careful not to scorch the salt in the process. This may take a few hours of careful monitoring. Turn off the heat once the water has evaporated and the salt is the consistency of wet sand.

DRY IT OUT

Transfer the salt into shallow baking trays and either put them out for the sun to dry it naturally or dry it out in an oven at a very low temperature. Evaporate any remaining moisture by transferring the salt to a clean cloth bag and hanging it for a few days.

ADD A PINCH

Once the salt is ready, you can grind it down to your preferred texture. Sprinkle it on your next meal to bring out the flavours, add ¼ cup to your bath to soothe aching muscles and stimulate your circulation or make a sea salt scrub (*see* page 198).

197

MAKE A SALT BODY SCRUB

Your skin is your body's largest organ and literally holds you together! It is protective and provides the sensation of touch. Sand, salt, sun and a gentle natural scrub can do wonders for your skin. Take some time to pamper it for a glorious glow.

GATHER

SEA SALT (*SEE* PAGE 196)

JAR OR CONTAINER

A CARRIER OR BASE OIL LIKE COCONUT, OLIVE OR ALMOND OIL

VITAMIN E OIL (OPTIONAL)

ESSENTIAL OILS OF CHOICE (OPTIONAL)

Your skin is constantly being renewed. The outer layer, or epidermis, regenerates every two to four weeks by shedding dead skin cells and replacing them with fresh new ones. You can speed up this natural process by exfoliating your skin.

The beach offers two of the most natural and effective exfoliants — sand and salt. Their grittiness helps dislodge old skin cells and unclog blocked pores, while the pressure from the scrubbing on your skin helps stimulate your circulation and lymphatic system, which is important for the immune system.

Making a sea salt body scrub takes a bit more time and effort, especially if you are harvesting your own sea salt (*see* page 196), but you can enjoy the experience and results in the comfort of your own home. Try these ideas for creating a salty, sensory skin delight.

ADD A SPLASH OF OIL

To make the salt into a scrub, grab a container and add ½ cup of sea salt and ½ cup of your preferred carrier oil. Adding oil to the salt forms an easy-to-apply paste and moisturises the skin as you exfoliate. A carrier oil (also known as a base oil) is used to dilute essential oils and 'carry' them to your skin. Carrier oils are usually vegetable oils derived from the seeds, kernels or nuts of a plant. Coconut, olive and almond oil are all good choices. It's important not to get your carrier oil and essentials mixed up, as essential oils are highly concentrated and can be harmful in large quantities. You may also like to add some vitamin E oil, a popular antioxidant known to nourish the skin and help it heal and repair.

CHOOSE YOUR SCENT

For some, the aroma of the oil and salt will be enough, but if you want to create a truly sensory spa experience, add a few drops of your favourite essential oil, such as vanilla or lavender, for a relaxing experience. Peppermint or citrus oils will be a bit more invigorating.

APPLY AND ENJOY

For the best results, use the scrub on damp skin, ideally after you have started your shower or while you are in the bath. Take handfuls of the scrub and gently massage it all over your skin in small circular motions. Take your time and really bask in the aroma and feeling of the scrub against your skin. Visualise the skin being renewed as you go. Once you're done, rinse it off, pat yourself dry and, for the ultimate glow, give your skin a big drink of your favourite moisturiser.

SCRUBBING AT THE BEACH

A sand scrub is a simple and easy option and can be applied before or after your swim. Simply get comfortable and grab a handful of sand. Gently massage it into your skin using small circular motions, and make your way slowly and mindfully from top to toe. Don't use too much pressure — it's meant to be relaxing and pleasurable — and avoid any areas where your skin might be irritated. Rinse it off in the sea and notice how soft your skin feels.

GAZE AT
THE STARS

Stars have long inspired awe and wonder, and they shine brightly above us all the time. Sunlight hides them during the day, but they're often visible at night. They're quite literally the stuff of myth and legend, and they can guide our navigation of the Earth and its oceans.

Only the brightest individual stars have been given names, but many others — cloud cover and haze dependent — are visible from Earth at night. The nearest star to the Earth is the sun.

Before the modern convenience of maps and global positioning system (GPS), people used the stars to chart their path across the seas — an ages-old science known as celestial navigation, or astronavigation. Ancient seafaring cultures followed the stars to explore and discover new territories. Polynesians used a type of celestial navigation called wayfaring, in which they interpreted information about the stars, sun, moon, planets, ocean and trade winds.

Indigenous Australians are the world's oldest living culture and have been using the stars to navigate for over 40,000 years. They do this in many ways, such as by following prominent stars, developing maps of the stars ('star maps') that correlate to landscape features and exploring the concept of cardinal directions. Much of the culture of the Warlpiri people in central Australia, for example, is based on four cardinal directions that correspond closely to Western cultures: north, south, east and west. In the Warlpiri culture, 'law' aligns with north, 'ceremony' with south, 'language' with west and 'skin' with east. 'Country' lies at the centre point of these directions and signifies 'here'.

Europeans, including the Vikings and ancient Greeks, also made huge advances in navigation and map-making by learning to recognise stars, like the North Star and constellations, along with their position relative to the horizon — as well as looking at the sun, longitude, latitude and, eventually, the compass (*see* page 114 to learn how to use and make a compass).

WHAT YOU SEE DEPENDS ON WHERE YOU ARE

Earth is located in the Milky Way galaxy, but when we look up at the stars, we all see a different sky. The stars and constellations vary depending on the hemisphere you're in, your location within that hemisphere and the seasons. Seek out the darkest skies to truly experience the night sky's vastness – go camping (*see* page 118), go on a microadventure (*see* page 100) or visit the ocean to see it stretching out before you — all the way to the horizon. A set of binoculars or a telescope will help you see even more.

UNDERSTAND THE NIGHT SKY

A star is a luminous sphere of plasma held together by its own gravity. When we're stargazing, we can think about stars as individuals, asterisms and constellations. What's the difference? An asterism is a recognisable pattern of stars grouped together — a bit like connect the dots. Asterisms then go on to form constellations, which outline and completely divide the sky into regions around central asterisms. For example, the seven brightest stars in the constellation Ursa Major comprise the asterism known as the Big Dipper. In western astronomy, there are 88 officially recognised constellations.

LOOK FOR PATTERNS IN THE SKY

Start by looking for familiar objects in the sky, such as the moon and Venus, and then practise identifying groups of stars or constellations. You can also use a star chart or an app to identify constellations in your hemisphere. Once you can recognise key stars and constellations, you'll be able to use them as reference points to locate others more easily.

201

NORTHERN HEMISPHERE — THE BIG DIPPER AND THE NORTH STAR

The Big Dipper is part of a constellation called Ursa Major. The Big Dipper has seven stars and is recognised as a grouping in many cultures. It is often described as looking like a bear, a wagon or a ladle and is found in the stories and legends of cultures around the world. A Native American legend tells the story of hunters who followed a bear into the sky, where you can still see this chase scene illustrated in the stars during long winter nights.

The Big Dipper's seven stars form the shape of a saucepan. Three of the stars form the handle, while the other four make up the pan itself. Once you've found it, you can locate the North Star, or Polaris, which always sits directly over the North Pole. In your mind's eye, imagine a line connecting the two stars that form the outermost edge of the Big Dipper's pan. Then follow this line to the upper right; the first bright star you come to is the North Star.

SOUTHERN HEMISPHERE — THE SOUTHERN CROSS AND THE SOUTH CELESTIAL POLE

The Southern Cross, or Crux, comprises four stars in the shape of a cross. The smallest of the 88 Western constellations, it was first described as a constellation in 1516 by an Italian explorer. For First Nations people in Australia, the Southern Cross represents one of many Dreamtime stories, and its symbolism varies across different Aboriginal communities.

You can use the Southern Cross to find the South Celestial Pole and due south. Once you've located its four stars, find the two pointers at the lower left, then envision a line between the pointers and a second line at a 90-degree angle to the one joining the two pointer stars. The South Celestial Pole is where that line meets the line created by the Southern Cross's two most widely separated stars. Finally, from the Pole, imagine dropping a line straight down to the horizon — that's south.

BE INSPIRED TO KEEP STARGAZING

There's a limit to what you can see with the naked eye and even with a good pair of binoculars. If you're inspired to explore further, seek out fellow stargazers and astronomers to view the stars through a telescope. Head to your nearest observatory or planetarium or find out if there are any night-sky tours near you.

Gazing at the stars is an incredible and humbling way to retain perspective of ourselves as singular beings and as a single civilisation on a single planet in a huge, vast and relatively unknown universe. It's also an awe-inspiring and ages-old way to retain our sense of humanity — we're all looking at the same sun, the same moon and the same stars as our ancestors were. We have looked to the stars for knowledge and understanding for millennia in our wild journey through life and — like much of this incredible planet we call home — there is still so much to learn. Keep stargazing and keep on growing, living and evolving a wild life.

THANK YOU

A big thank you to the community of people that were
part of the creation of *Wild Life*. Thank you to Hardie Grant,
Melissa Kayser and Amanda Louey who have believed in this book
since the beginning. Thank you to our writer Vanessa Murray who
always knows how to say it just right and talented wordsmiths
Georgia Gibson and Jeanie Watson. Thank you to the dedication
and hawk-eye talent of our editor Helena Holmgren
who always encouraged us to go deeper.

Thank you to all the organisations who have worked with
Design by Nature since 1999 and shared our vision for making this
beautiful planet more just and sustainable. Thank you to my
design colleagues Megan Edgoose and Kristin Soh for
your creativity and beautiful design skills.

Lastly, thanks to my family Nick, Tasman, Freya, Diana and Chris
for their unwavering support. And all my friends,
you know who you are — thank you!

ACKNOWLEDGEMENTS

Design
Anna Carlile
Megan Edgoose
Kristin Soh
designbynature.au

Writing
Vanessa Murray
Georgia Gibson
Jeanie Watson

PHOTOGRAPHY

Emilie Ristevski
@helloemilie, cover

Anna Carlile
designbynature.au
91, 157, 165, 167, 169, 171, 206

Alyson Morgan
@alysonsimplygrows
xiii, xiv, 5, 10, 26, 27, 34, 37,
58, 59, 66, 69, 79, 96

Marta Potoczek
martapotoczek.com
93

Ikebana Flowers, 61, 63
Planning, design, styling:
Anne Ladegast-Chiu,
Hilde
Floral Design: Carla Gottlieb,
Still Life Flowers
Photography: Claudia Gödke,
@claudiagoedke

Alamy
alamy.com
Premaphotos ,187
Imagebroker, 187
Arterra Picture Library, 187
Nick Gammon, 187

Flickr
flickr.com
Forest and Kim Starr, 71
Lukas Large, 138

iStock
istockphoto.com
VvoeVale, 125
Letizia Strizzi, 127
Dutchy, 128

Shutterstock
shutterstock.com
Adam Yee, 44
Anne Webber, 47

Iaksena, 71
Diana Taliun,71
Anna Gratys, 94
PaniYani, 95
Weha, 95
Franck Camhi, 99
Ninevija, 105
Heiko Kueverling, 138
Liz Seymour, 186

unsplash
unsplash.com
Hans Isaacson, iv
Paulo Freitas, 2
Priscilla Du Preez, 3
Abbie Bernet, 6
Pedro De Sousa, 7
Umit Yildirim, 8
Fiona Smallwood, 11
Eli Sivakova, 12
Dana Katharina, 14
Mitchell Hartley, 16
Beazy 19, 43
Ivana Cajina, 20
Joydeep Sensarma, 21
Annie Spratt, 23, 51, 55, 137
Ricardo Martins, 24
Donnie Rosie, 25
Michael Anfang, 28
Alexa Innhsg, 32
Lucas V, 33

ACKNOWLEDGEMENTS

Carlos Costa, 36
Laura Lauch, 38
Tim Wildsmith, 39
Luther Bottrill, 40
Scott Webb, 41
Feey Pflanzen, 44
Stephanie Pomerenke, 44
Chris Lee, 45
Content Pixie, 45
Lucian Alexe, 45
Pawel Czerwinski, 45
Fukayamamo, 48
Mor Shani, 49
Jacob Capene, 50
Adrien Delforge, 52
Gerrie Van Der Walt, 52
Edward Howell, 53
Joshua Lanzarini, 56
Stephanie Krist, 57
Mika Baumeister, 65
Daniel Krueger, 67
Kim Gorga, 70
Shelley Pauls, 70
Brittney Strange, 70
Robin Ooode, 72
Michael Tuszynski, 74
SirisVisual, 75
Mohit Pathak, 77
Jonathan Kemper, 81
Anna Hecker, 83
Julia Joppien, 84

Britt Gaiser, 88
Sophia Muller, 89
Lorenzo Ranuzzi, 94
Paul Morley, 94
Grigorii Sukhorukov, 95
Sasha Sashina, 100
Khushal Trivedi, 103
John Towner, 106
Olena Sergienko, 108
Joshua Earle, 109
Andy Mai, 110
Andrew Spencer, 113
Jamie Street, 115
Hendrik Morkel, 116
Kate Joie, 118
Andrea Zanenga, 119
Nathan Dumlao, 120
Jonathan Forage, 121
Mike L, 122
Ksenia Makagonova, 127
Abby Savage, 131
Robson Hatsukami Morgan, 133
Ian Keefe, 134
Timothy Meinberg, 135
Jessica Furtney, 140
Zoe, 142
Kees Streefkerk, 143
Adrien Olichon, 144
Ali Kazal, 145
Max Oh, 146

Barbara Verge, 147
Clay Banks, 148
Gigi, 151
Chris Yang, 153
Earl Wilcox, 154
Hans Isaacson, 154
Mauro Lima, 160
Danny Feng, 162
Isuru Ranasingha, 163
Tingfeng Xia, 172
Bogdan Ivanyshyn, 174
Rico Meier, 175
Stefan Stefancik, 176
Josh Roland, 179
Karl Fredrickson, 180
Benita Anand, 182
Shane Stagner, 185
Carlos Alberto Gomez Iniguez, 188
Mohamed Alaau, 190
Shifaaz Shamoon, 191
Bill Aboudi, 192
Wynand Uys, 195
Charles Deluvio, 197
Wil Stewart, 200
Jordan Steranka, 202
Guillaume Le Louarn, 204
Klemen Vrankar, 205

Published in 2022 by Hardie Grant Explore, an imprint of Hardie Grant Publishing

Hardie Grant Explore (Melbourne)
Wurundjeri Country
Building 1, 658 Church Street
Richmond, Victoria 3121

Hardie Grant Explore (Sydney)
Gadigal Country
Level 7, 45 Jones Street
Ultimo, NSW 2007

www.hardiegrant.com/au/explore

Publisher
Melissa Kayser

Project editor
Amanda Louey

Editor
Helena Holmgren

Proofreader
Lyric Dodson

Design
Design by Nature

Production coordinator
Jessica Harvie

Concept & Research
Anna Carlile

Writing
Vanessa Murray
Georgia Gibson
Jeanie Watson

Prepress and colour reproduction by Megan Ellis and Splitting Image Colour Studio

Printed and bound in China by LEO Paper Products LTD.

A catalogue record for this book is available from the National Library of Australia

Hardie Grant acknowledges the Traditional Owners of the Country on which we work, the Wurundjeri People of the Kulin Nation and the Gadigal People of the Eora Nation, and recognises their continuing connection to the land, waters and culture. We pay our respects to their Elders past and present.

Wild Life
ISBN 9781741178012

10 9 8 7 6 5 4 3 2 1

The paper this book is printed on is certified against the Forest Stewardship Council® Standards and other sources. FSC® promotes environmentally responsible, socially beneficial and economically viable management of the world's forests.